THE
MOON
+
YOU

Your Guide to Finding Energy, Balance,
and Healing with the Power of the Moon

DIANE AHLQUIST
Author of *Moon Spells*

ADAMS MEDIA
New York London Toronto Sydney New Delhi

Adams Media
An Imprint of Simon & Schuster, Inc.
100 Technology Center Drive
Stoughton, MA 02072

First Adams Media hardcover edition January 2020

ADAMS MEDIA and colophon are trademarks of Simon & Schuster.

For information about special discounts for bulk purchases, please contact Simon & Schuster Special Sales at 1-866-506-1949 or business@simonandschuster.com.

The Simon & Schuster Speakers Bureau can bring authors to your live event. For more information or to book an event contact the Simon & Schuster Speakers Bureau at 1-866-248-3049 or visit our website at www.simonspeakers.com.

Interior design by Sylvia McArdle
Interior images © 123RF/jaysi

Manufactured in the United States of America

3 2022

Library of Congress Cataloging-in-Publication Data
Names: Ahlquist, Diane, author.
Title: The moon + you / Diane Ahlquist, author of Moon Spells.
Description: Avon, Massachusetts: Adams Media, 2020.
Series: Moon magic.
Includes index.
Identifiers: LCCN 2019039417 | ISBN 9781507212141 (hc) | ISBN 9781507212158 (ebook)
Subjects: LCSH: Occultism. | Moon--Phases--Miscellanea.
Classification: LCC BF1623.M66 A34 2020 | DDC 133.5/32--dc23
LC record available at https://lccn.loc.gov/2019039417

ISBN 978-1-5072-1214-1
ISBN 978-1-5072-1215-8 (ebook)

The chocolate cake recipe in the Throw a Dinner Party entry and the frittata recipe in the Increase Plant-Based Protein Consumption entry are adapted from the following title published by Adams Media, an Imprint of Simon & Schuster, Inc.: *The Everything® Family Nutrition Book* by Leslie Bilderback, copyright © 2009, ISBN 978-1-59869-704-9.

DEDICATION

With great joy I would like to
dedicate this book to you,
my readers.

Remember to take care of yourself first,
then you can help others if they need it.

May you be inspired
by the phases of the moon
to work in harmony with her and always
shine your brightest!

CONTENTS

Chapter 1
FULL MOON 14

Chapter 2
WANING MOON 60

Chapter 3

DARK MOON 102

Chapter 4

NEW MOON 146

Chapter 5

☽ WAXING MOON 190

INTRODUCTION

Our connection with the moon is deep, meaningful, and powerful. Whether you find your body reacting differently at certain moon phases or notice changes in your mood, the effect of the moon on your body, mind, and spirit is unmistakable. And now, with *The Moon + You*, you'll learn quick, easy ways to harness that power.

Mother Nature has a huge impact on our lives on earth. If you choose to bond with her and let her speak to you, you will find that your life is more fulfilled and your well-being is improved. We never really know for sure what the weather will bring every month. But, the moon phases, which repeat, are remarkably consistent, with the exception of an eclipse here and there. That consistency gives us moon watchers the ability to plan ahead and receive all of the gifts we're being handed!

Just like the ebb and flow of tides on earth, your strong connection with the moon can help you bring in more of what you want and let go of what doesn't serve you. In these pages, you will find various activities, exercises, recipes, and thought-provoking ideas that align with the moon's phases to help you feel balanced, happy, and united with the universe at large. For example, a full moon calls us to be fearless and live with abundance, so try organizing a drum circle with friends. You'll want to release physical and emotional baggage during a waning moon, so that's the time to detox your skin and practice forgiveness. Consider fasting during part of the short time of a dark moon to rest and cleanse your body. A new moon celebrates beginnings, so smudge your home with a sage bundle and reenergize your crystal collection. The waxing moon encourages you to grow spiritually—it's a good time to write down your intentions and meditate on them. Each of the one hundred ideas will put you in sync with nature and let you put your mind, body, and spirit first.

Whether you're already enamored by the beauty and power of the moon or are just establishing a relationship with her, you can now use her energy with intention to improve your health and well-being. Each phase offers the potential for spiritual growth, personal development, and abundant happiness. Let the moon help you live your best life—one phase at a time.

HOW TO USE THIS BOOK

Using this book will awaken your senses and open your mind to the many ways the moon affects your life and how you can best harness its energy. Every phase offers specific wisdom and guidance that can help you, but you have to know how to best engage with its power at every step along its lunar path.

- **Full moon:** The moon is full in the sky, calling you to be fearless while you bask in its highest energy! This is the perfect time to try new activities, take a risk, and trust that it's going to work out for the best. The world is your oyster at this time, so embrace abundance and new opportunities, and start following your wildest dreams. Now's a good time to go out with a new person, open a business, or buy a new house. Full moon, full life!

- **Waning moon:** The moon appears to be getting smaller. In the Northern Hemisphere, which is half the planet, (including the USA, Canada, and so forth) it looks like a *D* (think *D* for decreasing for memory's sake.) In the Southern Hemisphere, it's reversed and looks like a *C*. This is a time to think about decreasing things in your life that are no longer serving you. This would be a great time to clean out your closets, basement, or garage, or cut ties with business dealings that haven't lived up to their hype. Minimize the physical and psychic clutter in your life.

- Dark moon: The moon's light disappears completely, and our intentions are set to rest, just for a few days. This is a time to withdraw and consider what's been serving you and what hasn't. It's not a time of preplanning for the new moon. It's simply time to be still and be present with what is.

- New moon: Showing just a sliver of light on the right. In the Northern Hemisphere, it looks like the right side of the capital letter *D*. In the Southern Hemisphere, it is reversed and it looks like a narrow letter *C*. Now's the time to start thinking about the fresh new lunar energy coming back into play. This is the time to contemplate anything you want to put into motion in the coming weeks—new activities, connections, hobbies, projects, or a business. Start making plans to take classes, network with new people, or buy new equipment.

- Waxing moon: This is a time of rebirth and regeneration as the moon makes its return to its full glory. As the moon's light increases, so does your personal power. Start setting your plans from the new moon into motion, keeping in mind that the full power of the moon is just around the corner—everything is coming your way right now!

Every section of this book will give you tips and activities to help you align your energy with the moon's so you can channel the power of the universe in your own life.

Chapter 1

FULL MOON

Everyone knows a full moon. It's usually most people's favorite because it's big, bold, and bright! Like its grand appearance, it has the biggest, boldest ability to empower you, as well. This is surely the most powerful lunar phase. This phase bestows upon you the motivation to try new things and to achieve goals that you have been wanting to fulfill. Your intuition is enhanced, and it's a time to project your highest intentions and focus on celebrating you.

The full moon is a creative time, so when you take time for yourself during this stage, you may want to tap into your artistic side or conjure up a remedy or two. Plan an event with friends and share the excitement or go solo and experience the vibration of the moon's light and potency. This phase has much to offer. Whether you are inside or outside, you will be exhilarated and inspired. Don't let this exceptional phase slip away without doing something special. It's more than just a phase—it's a lunar experience.

Meditate During a Full Moon

Meditation is a method of calm reflection that helps relieve stress and anxiety and improve your physical and spiritual well-being. Some people even meditate to try to achieve a heightened state of consciousness! When you meditate under a full moon (or on the day of a full moon), you'll experience especially powerful lunar energy. If you haven't meditated before, trying it during a full moon could be both fun and rewarding. If you're already proficient at meditating, you might be able to put yourself into an altered state more easily thanks to the intense lunar energy.

You only need a minimum of 10 minutes to do this full moon meditation. (Feel free to go longer, of course!) Follow these simple steps to find peaceful calm that can help rejuvenate your spirit:

- Dress comfortably. First, be sure you're wearing something comfortable and not binding.
- Find a suitable spot. Decide if you will meditate inside or out. Meditating in the full moonlight would be wonderful, but if you won't be comfortable, it's not worth it. You can still experience lunar energy inside, especially if you sit near a window.

- **Sit comfortably.** Do you want to sit on the floor or ground with your legs crossed? Or would you rather sit in a chair? Either way, be sure you will stay alert and not fall asleep. Maintain good posture, but don't be too stiff.
- **Close your eyes (if you want to).** Decide if you want to close your eyes or not. Some people like to see the space they're in; others like to close out the world and focus their attention inward. It's up to you!
- **Be in the present.** Check in with your senses. For example, pay attention to what you are hearing. Do you hear sounds of nature, soft music, the ticking of a clock? Be aware of what is going on around you.
- **Focus on your breathing.** Breathe naturally. Don't be concerned with how fast or slow you are breathing. As you focus, your breath will naturally slow down. Pay attention to the rhythm.
- **Be prepared for you mind to wander.** You may think of odd things like how you forgot to pay the electric bill or buy milk. It seems silly, but it's perfectly normal. Acknowledge these things and don't fight them. Then go back to focusing on your breathing.
- **Do a body scan.** You may start to feel different sensations within your body. Think about them, starting from your toes and working up. How do your toes feel? Do you feel air on them? Or are they warm thanks to the socks you have on? Make your way mentally up your body till you reach the top of your head. You don't want to try to adjust anything, just be aware of how your body feels.

- **Feel the full moon energy.** Now focus on the moon above, even if you are inside. What does it look like? How does it make you feel? Does it make you feel excited or curious? Think about how you are feeling now about this experience.
- **Come out of the meditation.** When you feel you have done enough, slowly open your eyes. If they are already opened, simply relax for a couple of seconds. Sit where you are until you feel the urge to leave your spot.

Each time you practice this meditation, you will feel and learn something new about yourself. You could jot down some notes after each time you do this meditation to track how you react to various full moons.

Visualize Artistic Pursuits

Everyone is artistic in some way. Even if it's not the way you make a living, you can most likely appreciate good art, food, music, and so on. You might even like to dabble in painting or listen to music in your free time as a way to relax and de-stress. On the other hand, you might be so passionate about the arts that you want to find or enhance a career in that area. (Be prepared for people around you to tell you to look for a "real job"! Try being a tarot card reader like me. That's even worse!) Whether you want to be creative as a hobby or a job, the full moon is here to lend a lunar hand. Your emotions are elevated during this phase, and from emotions come artistic endeavors. Ignite that inventive side of yourself and imagine your way to success.

You already use visualization when you daydream or imagine anything that has not yet come into fruition. In this exercise, you are going to be aware you are doing it as a means to an end. To make your imagining a springboard to attainment, simply use creative visualization techniques and free lunar power. Here, I present one method that is easy and effective.

- **Before you start, decide specifically what you want from your artistic pursuits.** Do you want to write and sing songs? If so, are you performing on stage or do you prefer to be in a recording studio? Do you want to paint small watercolors or string beaded jewelry to give loved ones as a personalized, handmade gift? Do you want to become a chef and open your own restaurant to create delicious dishes? Or do you want to work at the best restaurant in town and go home at the end of the day and not have the responsibility of being an owner? Be specific and honest with yourself. No goal is too small or too big. Write it down if you prefer. If you don't know specifically what you want, take time and think about it. If you are still not sure, start with one idea and see how that goes for you. But start with some type of specific direction. You can always change at another time.

- **Get comfortable.** On the night of the full moon, put something comfortable on and find a tranquil area where you can sit or lie down. It's best to be inside, as you will have your eyes closed and might even fall asleep. However, if you want to be outside, find a safe and comfortable area. Of course, don't forget to shut your phone and other screens off.
- **Create a specific mental image.** Using your imagination, ask yourself what you see once you are in the role you have chosen. What are you doing, hearing, wearing, and where are you? If there is an audience, is it large or small? Are you standing or sitting? Are you excited and motivated or calm and relaxed?
- **Repeat regularly.** Every day, find a few minutes to concentrate on this image or scene. You can do this when you first lie down at night or early in the morning—whenever time allows.
- **Add positive energy.** As you visualize your goal, see yourself happy within the image. If you smile or even laugh because you are so happy within your imagining, that's good…keep it positive.

After a while, visualizing this image will be part of your routine and you will be on the path to your artistic aspiration.

Work Out to Empower Yourself

Energy is racing on the day or night of a full moon, so why not let this powerful phase pump up your physique?

If you don't work out regularly, the full moon can motivate you to see what you can do! You might start with hiring a trainer for a session on the day or evening of a full moon and ask them to show you some basic exercises. If you'd rather exercise in a group, take a class at a YMCA or local gym as an experiment. Remember, ask for help before using machines or weights you're not familiar with.

If you are someone who works out frequently and you're up for a challenge, try some high-intensity interval training to burn fat during a full moon. I spoke with Bron Volney, a full-time fitness professional and NASM-certified personal trainer in Boston, Massachusetts. He advises skipping the exercise machines and instead create cardio through resistance training with light weights and body-weight exercises to strengthen your body as a whole.

Here is a simple sample workout to maximize full moon energy. You'll only need a couple of things:

- 1 pair of light dumbbells
- Jump rope

Here's what one set consists of:

- **30 seconds:** Wide-leg floor-reach stretch
- **30 seconds:** Squats

- **30 seconds:** Dumbbell curls for biceps (left side)
- **30 seconds:** Dumbbell curls for biceps (right side)
- **20 seconds:** Pushups
- **60 seconds:** Jump rope

- **30 seconds:** Butt kickers in place
- **30 seconds:** Downward Dog stretch
- **30 seconds:** Jumping jacks

Try to do three sets. No matter what exercise you choose, let the full moon be a springboard to creating a strong, healthy you.

Perform a Love Ritual to Attract a New Partner

When the moon is at its brightest, your love opportunities abound. Your intuition and romantic heart are amplified and at optimal performance. And so are your sexual impulses and passion! For something lasting, listen to your intuition. It will bring you clarity about attracting your romantic and caring vibrational match.

This ritual is always best done on the night of a full moon, as opposed to the day, as it's simply a more romantic time, and you want to encourage your feelings and emotions to come forth. Keep in mind, this ritual is to attract someone you don't know or have never met. It's not to get an old lover back or the guy or girl you work with to finally ask you out. Let the universe send you someone. Have faith! Here's what you will need:

- Some cardboard, a paper plate, or just a couple of pieces of paper
- Pen or pencil
- A pink envelope, if you have one; if not, a white one will do

1. Perform this ritual inside unless you are comfortable and safe being outside. Make sure you are not distracted—turn your phone and other screens off. If you like, play music. Light your favorite candles (a yellow candle is a good choice, as it attracts) or keep lights dim.

2. Cut out two figures from your cardboard or paper. One will represent you, and the other, someone you will be attracting to you. Don't worry about what your figures look like—just trust that what you're making is correct. If you can't create figures at all, just cut a strip, write *Me* on one and *He*, *She*, or *Partner* on the other.

3. Place everything in front of you. Now say the following: "At this full moon so bright and sweet, I call to you so that we meet. We both will know this is the one. Bring love and light and moonlit fun."

4. Put your figures in the envelope in a place of dignity and somewhere you deem special.

> "At this full moon so bright and sweet, I call to you so that we meet. We both will know this is the one. Bring love and light and moonlit fun."

Wait till the next full moon and see if you have met someone or if you are receiving signs that someone is on the way. A sign may be anything that is associated with love. For example: You find that heart-shaped locket you lost, or maybe a book that you associate with romance falls off your shelf out of the blue.

Try to look at your envelope every day, even if it's just a glance for a couple of seconds. If you choose to, you can take the figures out to look at them, but it's not necessary. Trust that the full moon will be bringing some passion into your life.

Raise Your Vibrational Energy

We are vibrational beings. The molecules that make up your body are constantly vibrating—sometimes slower, sometimes faster, depending on your mood and health. The molecules are likely to move slower if you are down in the dumps and constantly reinforcing that narrative to yourself. If you are positive and upbeat with yourself and others, your vibrational energy is likely to be higher. Since what you put out into the world comes back to you, it's a good idea to put out high vibrational energy. You create your own reality, so pay attention to how you think, what you think, and start to make small changes, such as doing exercises like this one. The more you begin to see changes for the better in your life, the more you will believe you have the ability to lift yourself vibrationally…because you are already controlling it. (Of course, if difficult thoughts persist, talk to your healthcare provider.)

Use this exercise on the day or night of a full moon (morning is better in this case, as you can start the entire day on a good note) to raise your vibration when you're feeling sluggish. It's well suited for the morning while you're still in bed because you are in a sort of altered state of consciousness, or what some might call half asleep. The day has not started, emails and texts have not been read, and no one in the house or at work has started complaining yet. Take advantage of this blank slate! If possible, set aside 15 minutes for this process and try to do it daily or at least twice a week. You don't have to think of it as a meditation unless you want to. Start doing it during a full moon because it's easier to jump-start routines during this phase. Then you can keep it going during all moon phases.

1. On the morning of a full moon, wake up naturally if you have time or set your alarm for 15 minutes earlier than normal if you're on a schedule. Stay in bed. If you are going to do this later in the day, just get comfortable any way you see fit.

2. Be grateful and think about what you have. You have so much. Examples are, "I have a roof over my head," "I have food," or "I have a great haircut" (yes, you can be shallow sometimes). The idea is to switch your thoughts from what you *don't* have to what you *do* have that is good. The more you focus on what you don't have, the more the universe will give more of what you don't have.

3. Now think about what you would like to see happen of a positive nature today. At this point, only think of things you feel are possible. "I would like to see a bag of money on my sink when I get up to brush my teeth" may not be a good choice. Work in baby steps. Try, "I will have no problem getting a seat on the bus today," "At lunch I will get that window view," or "My cat will finally eat that healthy cat food I bought." Visualize yourself on the bus, at lunch, or having your cat give you a paws up for the cat food to help solidify the idea in your mind.

4. After you start to see success with your smaller ideas, expand on them and focus on larger things, like raises, trips, wellness, and relationships.

Before you know it, you will be really in tune with your vibrational energy and able to shift your thoughts from lack to abundance in just a few minutes!

Do a Moon Salutation Yoga Routine

You may have heard of the yoga sequence called Sun Salutation, which is often practiced first thing in the morning and is designed to awake and invigorate. It has a counterpart, Moon Salutation, which is designed to cool down and quiet the mind. Full Moon Salutations are considered particularly useful when energies are high and you need to slow down your body and soul. For this reason, it's best to do these poses in the evening. And if you can get out into the light of the full moon, so much the better.

There are many variations of Moon Salutations, and one is not essentially better than the other. On a physical level, you will be stretching all your muscle groups and increasing flexibility. You are also improving your respiratory, circulatory, and digestive systems. Follow this sequence of basic yoga poses:

- **Namaste:** Start with a simple Namaste by bringing your hands into prayer position in front of you. This is an acknowledgement of the divine in yourself and in everyone and everything around you.
- **Goddess Squat:** Place your feet more than hip-width apart and take a deep breath as you descend into a gentle squat. Raise your arms straight up, then fold your elbows at a 90-degree angle and rotate your arms so your palms face forward. Hold the pose for a few seconds and breathe.

- Star: Come up from your goddess squat but keep your legs apart, feet facing forward. Extend your arms outward, parallel to the ground. With your palms facing down, spread your fingers wide and hold.
- Triangle, right side: Rotate your right foot so that it's at a right angle to your ankle, pointing outward. Keeping your hips forward, bend toward your right foot and place your right hand on your right ankle while raising your left hand to the sky. Breathe deeply into this pose.
- Pyramid, right side: Rotate your body toward your right leg, point your left foot in the same direction as your right foot, and fold your body over the right leg, keeping your back parallel to the floor. Bring your hands together behind you, over your lower back.
- Triangle, left side: Point your right foot forward and rotate your left foot so that it's at a right angle to your ankle, pointing outward. Keeping your hips forward, bend toward your left foot and place your left hand on your left ankle while raising your right hand to the sky.
- Pyramid, left side: Rotate your body toward your left leg, point your right foot in the same direction as your left foot, and fold your body over the left leg, keeping your back parallel to the floor. Bring your hands together behind you, over your lower back.

- **Goddess Squat**: Place your feet more than hip-width apart and take a deep breath as you descend into a gentle squat. Raise your arms straight up, then fold your elbows at a 90-degree angle and rotate your arms so your palms face forward. Hold the pose for a few seconds and breathe.
- **Standing Mountain Pose**: Bring your feet a bit closer together and stand up tall. Bring your hands together again in prayer pose. Take a deep breath and end with another Namaste.

Remember, the full moon is a time of completion—the skies have been building up to this phase. For men and women who are especially stressed out, tired, and "heated up" for one reason or the other, it will give you a cooling yoga flow. It's moon rejuvenation and balance at their best.

Moisturize Your Skin

The full moon is the peak time to rejuvenate your skin, as the moon's energy is at maximum momentum and your skin absorbs with more gusto. For this exercise, you'll need to start ahead of time to find out when the next full moon is. Then, you can consider how you want to take care of your skin during that time, depending on your preference and budget:

- **Book an appointment for that day at a spa for a facial or for an entire beauty treatment.** Let someone else do the work while you bask in the full moon energy. Make sure you get a moisturizing treatment, as your skin loves being hydrated under the influence of this lunar queen. It just absorbs so much more easily.
- **Make an appointment with yourself to do your own procedures at home.**

A face mask is an easy and effective way to moisturize your skin at home. There are many options on the market, so take time to investigate your skin type and ingredients that work best for you. While your mask is hardening or setting or doing its magic, soak your feet in Epsom salt or buy a foot soak and feel the bubbles soothing your toes. (Your feet need moisture too!) When finished, gently dry your feet and rub moisturizer on them.

Bring to mind the vitality of the full moon while you enjoy your relaxing treatments. It's enhancing everything you do.

Charge Bottles of Water

To create a bit of lunar momentum that can continue after the full moon passes, try making your own full moon energy drink. There are no fancy labels, you won't see a commercial with your favorite celebrity holding it, and you won't find it on the Internet. There are no flavors, so you don't have any stress making a choice, but there also aren't any preservatives or chemicals. Just charge it and drink up!

Want to bathe in your energy drink? Go ahead. Pour some into your bathwater and be rejuvenated. It's all about your intention. You are in charge of the charge! You are tapping into the life-giving properties of water and the energy of the full moon's influence, which can serve many purposes. Even your plants and vegetables will be screaming, "Do me next!" It will bring an organic smile to your leafy pals.

To charge your water, grab some safe drinking water. It could be your favorite bottled water, a gallon jug, or good tap water. Put the under the light of the full moon. If you can't put it outside, put the water somewhere near a window or door where you can at least see the sky even if you can't see the moon. If that's not possible either, visualize the moon above or get a picture of a full moon and put the water in front of that. Now you're ready for the charging ritual:

1. Once your water is in position, take both your hands and hold them above and over the water. Close your eyes and see the radiance of the full moon coming down toward your hands. Visualize your hands as a filter and allow the

light to penetrate your hands and hit the water. (Even if you have twenty bottles of water, your hands can spiritually cover them all.)

2. Focus on that image for a few seconds, until you feel the water has shifted and is infused with force.

3. Now take your water and store it where you normally would keep it.

If you want to try something extra fun, do a full moon water experiment with friends. (This experiment can be done any time as long as the water has been charged on the day or night of the full moon.) Don't disclose anything about the moon, or charging, or any clue at all. Put a small glass (about 3 ounces) of regular water and the same amount of moon-charged water in front of someone and ask them to try both and tell you which water tastes better. If they chose the moon-charged water, they are full moon sensitive. If not, the worst that you did is hydrate them, and that's always a good thing!

Organize a Drum Circle with Friends to Celebrate Abundance

First off, what is a drum circle? A drum circle is a term used to describe a group of people usually from a surrounding communities who come together to play percussion instruments (especially hand drums) in order to experience healing and spiritual fulfillment. It's rhythm or music therapy for those in attendance. Musical percussion can affect us on a mental, physical, and spiritual level thanks to its intense vibrations, which you can hear and feel. You can drum with intention—for general well-being, for example, or a specific reason upon which your group has decided in advance.

Public drum circles have become very dramatic in some areas. They may include belly dancers, jugglers, and just about all styles of performers. However, you won't find electronic keyboards, electric guitars, or regular drum sets (or you shouldn't)—drum circles should be connected to nature as much as possible. That's why a full moon drum circle is so popular. It captures the excitement of the full moon, even if you're inside.

First, decide how many people you want to invite to your drum circle. This will determine the location. If you have several people in mind already, great. But what if you want to try it alone first? No worries, you can drum by yourself and still lift your vibration. Just sit and visualize yourself as part of a circle. (Don't sit *inside* the circle…you are *part* of the circle!)

If you have a group in mind, decide where to hold it. Perhaps you could rent a room at a local community center or outdoor location. If you prefer to have it at your home, that's fine too. No matter where you have it, be sure that everyone has something to drum, clink, or make a noise. People can bring their own instruments, or you can provide them if that works better for your group. You can use something as simple as a pot or cardboard box and a wooden spoon or as elaborate as tribal drums made in Africa.

You should also think about who in your group could be the facilitator. The facilitator starts the drumming, keeps a beat, and tells everyone when to stop.

Once everyone has their instrument, assemble people in a circle. A circle is an important formation because represents source energy, balance, protection, and power. The facilitator should then announce the group's intention. For example, let's use finances. Set your goals in advance by telling everyone to visualize their financing growing as the music grows. (That doesn't mean you should beat the heck out your drum simply to get more money. Just drum slowly and steadily and think or "see" money falling into the circle or yourself smiling because your checking account is advancing in numbers.)

The facilitator should begin drumming. Then, the next person in the circle repeats the beat and adds something of his/her own. We all have rhythm, believe it or not. Even if you make one shake of a tambourine or one thump on the pot, you're bringing up energy in the room.

The facilitator should be the one to end the session after a given amount of time that all decided on before you began by saying something like, "We are ending our session now; let's all stand." When you all stand, each person can give a one-word observance of the session, such as "beautiful," "inspiring," "strange," etc. You'll probably hear a range of answers!

Some additional tips for organizing a drum circle:

- Don't try to outplay someone else and don't show off!
- Don't smoke in a drum circle.
- Don't wear rings if you are using someone else's drum.

Experiment with this activity and see what you come up with. We all hear a different drum.

Clearing and Charging Gemstones and Crystals

The powerful energy of a full moon is a perfect time to clear and purify your crystals and gemstones, whether they're raw or polished stones, decor, or jewelry. First, you want to clear any previous energy or intentions associated with the stone, then you can charge it with your own.

Start by clearing it of the energy of others who may have handled the stone before you. Note that sometimes stones or materials near them (like necklace cords) are not water tolerable, so check before you immerse anything. Here are a few different methods to clear stones:

- If you live near any body of water, even a swimming pool, you can dip the stone in the water and envision gray smoke (representing the negative tension) coming out of the stone. If you don't have access to a body of water, run the stone under the tap and imagine the same thing.
- Fill a small bowl with water and add a dash of table salt. This combination will rid the stone of contamination and impurities.

- Smudge your stones, as talked about in the Smudge and Bless Your Home activity in Chapter 4.
- Give them a soapy scrub with a gentle detergent. While I do this, I keep the water running and imagine any bitter energy picked up by the piece swirling down the drain. You can clear as many stones as you want at a time.

Now your piece of jewelry or gemstone is cleared and ready to go. The next step is to charge it for protection. Charging a gemstone simply means stimulating or refreshing its natural ability to direct energy. To do this, leave your piece in the light of a full moon for the night and retrieve it the next day. If you can't leave it outside, place it on a windowsill and just know the moon's light is reaching it.

When you feel it has the full moon charge, hold it and give it a hint of what it's supposed to do. Put together your own words or say something like, "Safeguard me from negativity," or "Protection."

An interesting note about crystal care: If a gemstone occasionally chips or breaks, it is doing its job. It's taking psychic hits for you and protecting you from people, places, and things that may not have your best interest at heart.

Create a Meditation To-Go Bag

To meditate, all you really need is your mind, body, and spirit, and luckily, you have those things with you all the time. But if you prefer to have a few other things on hand when you meditate, you might want to assemble a small bag of meditation items that you can grab and use on the go. After all, you still need to take care of yourself when you're on the move for one reason or another! Whether you travel for work a lot, stay at a friend's house once in awhile, or are just going from one end of the house to the other, why not be prepared?

First, find a bag or case of some type, such as a tote or small zippered bag. Think about where you are going most often and how you get there—do you want something that stands on its own or fits in another bag? You might want to collect the items to put in the bag first, then decide what type of bag can hold them all easily and conveniently. Here are some things to consider including in your to-go bag:

- **Something to sit on**: A round beach towel is a great option. (Yes, they do sell them.) Look for one with an interesting designs, like perhaps a mandala, which is a Sanskrit word for a circle or center filled with shapes and patterns (I've seen these for around $25). If that type of towel won't work for you, use a yoga mat, regular beach towel, or whatever suits you.

- **Music:** For something easy and portable, download meditative music on your cell phone. If you prefer old-school CDs, be sure you have a device to play them on.
- **Candles:** Votive candles in a jar are perfect for a to-go bag. You can get them at a dollar store in a jar with a twist-off lid in a variety of scents. (Don't forget matches or a lighter.) Remember, colors have different vibrations so choose a color based on your needs:
  - **Blue:** Tranquility
  - **Pink:** Love
  - **Purple:** Psychic pursuits
  - **White:** Purity, peace (when in doubt use white)
- **Incense:** Pack your favorite incense in a container you can seal. (You don't want to end up scenting everything in your bag forever.) And please be sure you have permission to light incense wherever you are staying, whether it's a friend's house or a hotel.
- **Statues:** You can even create a makeshift altar on the road if you like. Bring your favorite statue of a goddess, saint, Buddha, etc.
- **Gemstones:** Bring your favorite gemstones, but remember, they can be weighty so keep that in mind if you'll be carrying your bag by hand. Remember, you can always wear gemstones as jewelry around your neck or as a pin or bracelet.

Once you have all your articles in your bag, it's time to call on the authority of the full moon to activate this meditation gear. What you'll be doing is heightening the vibration of every item in the bag so you can ease into a meditate state more readily and have a more successful session each time you meditate. To charge your to-go bag, follow these steps:

1. On the night or day of a full moon, put the bag on a windowsill or anywhere it may be in the view of the moon. If that is not possible, you can put it in front of a full moon picture or draw a circle representing a moon and place it in the bag.
2. Take a few minutes and visualize light coming down from the moon and entering your bag.
3. Let it sit to charge for as long as you feel.
4. Now you are ready to go. It sounds simple, but you are in fact appealing to your subconscious through this process.

Making this bag is well worth the effort, as being organized makes it more likely that you'll keep up your meditation practice when you're on the go.

Celebrate Unions by Planting Trees

Trees are symbolic of many things, but what I love most is that they represent putting down roots. When you plant a tree during a full moon, that energy embodies completion and growth—therefore, you have an enchanting occasion for the joining together of two people or even families. You could also celebrate the starting of a new business, home, or idea.

Planting a tree to celebrate a union is an ancient tradition. It represents growth, strength, and longevity. Full moons inspire romantic vibrations and are a time of conclusion or the finality of a union. Planting a tree is a delightful way to celebrate getting married or renewing vows or making a big commitment of some kind. If you are mixing two families, everyone can contribute to the ceremony. Here's one way to hold a tree ceremony. You will need:

- A small tree (indigenous or earth friendly to where it's being planted…don't plant a palm in Alaska) already in a pot that has a special meaning to the couple. You can also consider tree symbology:
  - Use a tree that brings back a happy memory, such as meeting by an evergreen
  - Fruit trees: A fruitful union
  - Lilac: Honesty and new beginnings
  - Myrtle: True and everlasting love

- 2 small buckets of soil
- 2 small gardening trowels (little shovels)
- Water in a watering can or pitcher
- 2 hand towels or wet wipes to clean your hands

1. Have the couple stand next to each other or across from each other or have the group stand together. The overseer now says, "This full moon tree planting ceremony represents the union between _____ and _____. The full moon represents their _____ (say something about the bond, such as, 'Powerful love for each other and the strength of their promise' or 'The strength of this idea and the power of its ability to help others'). It represents them setting down roots and withstanding all weather they may encounter in their partnership. May it grow high and strong."

2. He/she continues to say, "Now each of you take your soil at the same time and put it on the base of the tree." Then have each one pour a little water on the soil. It doesn't matter who pours the water first.

3. Have the couple say an ending statement that suits them. "And so it is," "Amen," "Blessings," and so forth.

As a gift, someone may want to give the people involved aprons, the shovels, or a watering can to decorate themselves. After the ceremony, the couple or group should plant the tree or place it on a balcony or spot that they have chosen.

Plant Air-Purifying House Plants

The expression is, "Keep the house green and the air clean." Where do you think the air is cleaner—in a city or in a forest? You guessed it… the forest. Back in 1989, Dr. Bill Wolverton, a former NASA research scientist, conducted a landmark plant study in which he determined that the bigger the leafy surfaces, the better the air purification qualities of that plant. House plants are natural air purifiers! Goodbye lilac-scented cans of air freshener, and hello real breathing, loving, areca palms.

Toxic compounds live all around us—in upholstery, cleaning products, garages, places with poor ventilation. Let's clean the air with plants that look good and do good in your home—your lungs, your home, and the planet will thank you.

A full moon is a great time to plant these little friends who can heal us, absorb pollutants, and transmit healthy air instead of harmful toxins. The moisture caused by the pull of the moon is moving upward into the leaves of your inside plants. Here is a short list of inside plants that are good air purifiers. Use these ideas as a start, but ask your doctor and local horticulturist what other options might work well:

- **Areca palms:**Removes toluene, which is found in contact cement, nail polish, and lacquer, and removes that specific smell of paint thinner.

- **Garden mums (chrysanthemum):**They remove ammonia, benzene, and formaldehyde while in bloom. When done blooming, plant them outside.
- **Aloe plants:**This plant is magic to me. It not only soothes sunburns, itching, cuts, and stings, but can also purify air pollutants from cleaning products.
- **Snake plant:**This houseplant doesn't need much light or water. Your kind of plant? It is efficient at absorbing carbon dioxide and releases oxygen at night. (Most plants release oxygen during the day.) So, if you place this plant in the bedroom, you may get a better night's sleep!

To make things easy on yourself, buy a plant already started and replant it the day or night of a full moon. (You can start from seedlings, but you need to plan ahead and be patient!) Once you have a plant:

1. Find a vessel you like that has drainage.
2. Fill it with good-quality soil.
3. Read the instructions on the plant's needs and follow them. Some inside plants need sun, some don't. What does the label say or what does the professional at the garden store say? Take their advice.

Keep your home green and breathe healthier. With just a little plant and a little love, you'll experience a whole lot of better breathing.

Make an
Abundance Bracelet

You are probably wondering why making a bracelet during a full moon is any different than making one at another time of the month. It's because it's charged by full moon energy, and that makes it magical. Don't believe it? I wouldn't have blamed you until I tried it. You're going to make a bracelet for you to wear that will bring good things to the people you think about while you make it. It's for healing, happiness, awakening, and even material things they may desire. Oh, and I haven't forgotten you. You get good things from it too!

In advance of the full moon or early on that day allow enough time to gather up what you need.

Look around the house to see if you can come up with items that can be repurposed into charms for a bracelet: old buttons, a broken piece of jewelry that has a bead or such on it, seashells with holes, old key rings, little charms, and so forth. There are no rules here. If you think it will work or has special meaning and can be hung on a piece of elastic…use it. Each bead or trinket will represent a person you want to help (plus one for yourself). For example, if you should find a bead or charm that reflects that person or you can make it reflect that person in the way you think about them. If Larry likes to fish, and you want him to heal from something, you might represent him with a seashell or something blue that represents the sea. Try not to go over ten people to keep the bracelet at a manageable length. You may want to also write these intentions down so you remember what it all meant later. (Don't worry too much about the weight or aesthetics—you only wear this bracelet for 15 minutes.) If you absolutely can't find anything for your bracelet in your home, you may have to take a trip to the hobby store, thrift store, or grandma's attic.

Next, you will need a piece of string, elastic, leather cord, or anything the pieces you have chosen will pull through. Begin stringing the items onto the bracelet. With each item you string, think of what that person wants.

When you're done stringing them together, tie a knot. Holding your wrist with bracelet toward that full moon, say, "Send everyone my good intentions and an abundance of love." You can add to that or make up your own sentiment. Wear the bracelet for 15 minutes or longer to project your intention to the universe, and then take it off and store it somewhere safe. If you have to cut if off and it falls apart, just keep the parts in a baggie or box. When all get what they want, dispose of the items or reuse them for something else.

Also, consider including others if you would like to make this a group activity. Have a Full Moon Bracelet Ceremony by creating a party atmosphere or inviting a few friends over. Maybe one person can bring a box of old beads, another elastic or cord, and another some snacks. You can enjoy each other's company while making your own bracelets.

Recite Healing Chants

You can use the power and brilliance of the full moon to take a good look at whatever is dragging you down and start to correct it by using one of the most ancient and primal forms of healing: chanting.

Chanting dates back to ancient times and some consider it to be the first form of singing as well as a way to prepare for meditation. It can soothe both your soul and body. The following examples are Buddhist chants. The simple act of repeating one resonant phrase over and over can lower your blood pressure, ease anxiety, help you focus, improve creativity, and connect you to the universe. (Try getting all of that in one over-the-counter medication!)

There is a chant for virtually any issue or problem that you want to address in your life. Let's talk about a few here, keeping in mind that you can easily find more with a simple search online:

- **Om mani padme hum**: Associated with the Buddha of Compassion. There are different literal translations, but all of them center on a jewel in the lotus. Repeat this chant to soothe worries, connect with your higher self, and heal old emotional wounds.
- **Aham aarogyam**: Use this chant to generate better health. This translates to, "I am healthy."
- **Om shanti shanti shanti**: This is a chant used in Buddhism as well as Hinduism to invoke peace. *Om* is the representation of consciousness. Repeating *shanti* three times brings peace to your body, soul, and words.

Before you begin your chant, take time to prepare a soothing space. Chanting is a peaceful practice, and it requires a certain amount of focus. It would be ideal for you to be outdoors under the light of the full moon, but if there is a lot of cloud cover, or it happens to be below zero where you live, practice your chants near a window and do the following:

1. Put a blanket on the ground so that you can connect with the earth. Find a comfortable position.
2. Choose your chant for its intended purpose. If you aren't sure how to pronounce the words, try an Internet search.
3. Sit quietly and meditate on the issue(s) you're seeking healing for. What does the perfect healing/solution look like in your imagination?
4. Hold this vision while you take three deep breaths and begin your chant. Let the sound come from deep in your abdomen and feel it resonate in your chest and throat.
5. Repeat your chant slowly until you feel relaxed and in tune with your spirit and intention, keeping your visualization of healing in your mind's eye the entire time.
6. Bask in the light of the full moon, knowing that its power lifts your intention to its highest level.

Some people like to use prayer beads to keep track of their chant recitations. Others like to add chimes, Tibetan singing bowls, or other types of soothing sound to their practice. Don't be afraid to experiment!

Read Your Own Aura
with a Mirror

An aura is an energy field that surrounds all physical and astral bodies. Auras have colors associated with them that can be seen by special photography or anyone willing to learn about them. As your emotions change, so do your auras. Using two moon phases—full and dark—let's see how your aura may change. You will need a notebook or journal to document what you see.

1. One the day or night of the full moon, sit or stand in front of a fairly large mirror. Do it at a time when you are alone inside and have no one watching, a peaceful time. Stare at the middle of your forehead (your third eye).
2. After focusing at that spot for approximately 30 seconds, look at the area with your peripheral vision. Remember to keep your focus on the spot in the center of your forehead.
3. Keep concentrating. You should see the background directly behind yourself becoming brighter and more in focus than the backdrop. This is your aura. It will become clearer the more you focus. You might see one or two colors at first, or several.
4. Now, write in your journal what you see. Document the date and that it is a full moon.

Most people have one or two colors that dominate their aura. Ordinarily, the brighter and more vivid the aura, the healthier and more spiritually evolved you are. Following are the basic colors and their meanings.

- **White:** This is actually *light*, not white. We are actually speaking of light, not pigment. White is always a positive vibration. We should strive for light, not white. But most people tend to use the word *white*.
- **Red:** Physical body. It can indicate force, energy, and stamina. Someone self-centered, materialistic, athletic, or sexual.
- **Orange:** Thoughtfulness, self-control, and optimism. People who are uplifting, like the sun. Sometimes they have issues of trust.
- **Yellow:** Well-being and wisdom. Such people absorb information easily and essentially enjoy life.
- **Green:** Good listener, focusing on healing the self and others. This is the color of various types of healers.
- **Blue:** The color of the spirit, meditation, and truth. All shades of blue are good. Artistic people tend to have blue in their auras. Sometimes they can be a bit melancholy (as in, "I'm feeling blue today").
- **Purple:** The most mystical of all the colors. It represents spirituality, intuition, nature, and seekers. This color does not linger too long. Often you will see it settle into a deep blue. It signifies that you have spiritual thoughts and insights at the time. The full moon should show more purple than the dark moon.

- **Black:** Black has both good and bad qualities, and, hence, it can be confusing. The negative is hate, depression, evil. The positive side is it can mean protection. Sometimes if someone is fearful, they will emit a black aura as a form of protection.

Check your aura again in the same way on the night of the dark moon and note the differences. See what has happened in your life between the full moon and the dark and see if you can make any connections between events and colors.

Journal and Freewrite to Gather Insight

During this time of illumination, take some time to reflect and gather insight. Sit quietly, clear your mind, center yourself, and make a connection with the divine.

During the full moon, our full power comes to light (pun intended). Now is the time to dig deep into your thoughts and dreams, to pull out insight that has long been buried under daily worry, self-doubt, lack of motivation, or any other kind of barricade you might subconsciously throw in your own path. This is the phase where you can connect with the universe, with your own divinity, and rediscover who you are underneath all of the clutter and noise of life.

Journaling is a great way to get your thoughts out of your head for examination. It allows you to not only follow through on a train of thought but to reread your ideas and perhaps come away with a better understanding of them. During the full moon, some things to journal about are:

- **Creative interests:** Are you feeling the need to paint, dance, draw, tell stories?
- **Personal connections:** Are they working or is there something holding you back in your relationships?
- **Finances:** What are your long-term goals? How do you intend to achieve them?

- Work:Are you satisfied and challenged or are you feeling stuck?
- Fitness:Do you want to get stronger and healthier? Are you motivated by wanting better health, wanting to look better in your clothes, or by something else entirely?

Freewriting is a fun exercise to try during the full moon. (Take note: This is not the same as *automatic writing*, which is a psychic tool and involves connecting with entities and spirits.) This type of writing is intended to help your thoughts simply flow for 10-15 minutes. Start by sitting quietly and reflecting on your connection with nature and your spirituality. Then ask yourself what you want to experience during the full moon. What is calling to you? What is seeking you? What do you want clarity on?

1. Let your thoughts about this simply come to you and write without worrying about grammar, spelling, punctuation, or even meaning.
2. If you feel like you're stuck and have nothing to say, keep writing. This is part of the exercise, writing without stopping. You can write about feeling stuck until another clear thought comes to you.

Don't worry if much of what you've written seems like gibberish. The point of the exercise is to pull the coherent parts of your writing and to focus and expand on those elements in a more structured entry. Who knows? You might become a full-fledged, full moon writer!

Learn about Others Through Body Language

We all know that our nonverbal cues give off intense energy. You've likely been in the situation where someone is saying one thing, but the way they're looking (or not looking) at you, the way they're standing, the way their body is moving is in complete disagreement with their spoken word. And because energy does not lie, we tend to pick up on this pretty easily—whether we listen to our instincts in the moment is a whole other issue.

During the full moon, everyone's energy tends to run high, which makes it a little easier for you to study body language. All those little unintentional motions are on full display! This is a good time to start honing in on nonverbal cues and deciding for yourself whether they match what someone is saying. This is a fun learning activity, and you can use it in every face-to-face interaction you have, whether you're talking to your partner, your child, a clerk at the grocery store, or your boss. Here are some of the obvious cues to watch for:

- **Eye contact:**When someone is having a hard time looking you in the eye, deception is most likely afoot, or they just can't bring themselves to dive into a tough conversation.
- **Hands to the face:**When someone is lying or deceiving you in some way (they might not technically be lying, but

they're also not offering up the truth you're asking for), it's common for their hands to rise to their face, usually around the mouth. They may rub their chin or actually put their fingers on their lips.

- **Touch or rub to the back of the neck:** Another sign of deception. This is thought to arise from a need to comfort oneself, a way to say, "Hey, it's all right you're a stinking liar."
- **Crossed arms:** This one is a little trickier. It's sometimes said to be a classic sign of someone not being open to a conversation, but honestly, some people just find this position comfortable, so assess carefully and look for other cues.
- **Jumpy feet:** When someone is bouncing a leg or jiggling their feet while seated, they're clearly antsy. The question is why? Look for other cues (like averted eyes) to clarify what's going on. It could be that the person has been sitting in a meeting for a long time and is just bored, but if you're asking your teenager where s/he was all night, this cue means something entirely different (read: They are nervous!).

There are scores of other indicators that you can find from reputable sources such as *The Everything® Body Language Book* by Shelly Hagen, which offers great insights in an easy-to-read format. And while the full moon is a wonderful time to study body energy on display, be careful with people whose body language is rehearsed—someone like a politician or a CEO rarely makes a mistake with body language, so they may be tougher to read.

Indulge In a Therapeutic Bath with Homemade Bubbles

Give honor to your body by the light of the full moon. The full moon can make some people more sensitive and aware of their emotions and those people need to be sure to make time to relax during this phase. Whether you are especially sensitive to the energy of the full moon or not, it's a good time to find some form of relaxation and a healthy bubble bath is a sure cure.

A bubble bath is a gift of sorts to yourself, as you are indulging in a self-care ritual. Light some candles or at least have low lighting and add soft music. Then gather:

$\frac{1}{2}$ cup distilled water

$\frac{1}{2}$ cup unscented castile liquid soap (named after olive oil–based soaps that originated in Castile, Spain and can also be made of other natural oils such as almond, hemp, avocado, and walnut)

$\frac{1}{4}$ cup vegetable glycerin

5 drops lavender oil or your favorite essential oil (optional)

Amethyst crystal (optional)

1. Pour these ingredients into a jar, jug, or some type of vessel.
2. Take your mixture and charge it by letting it sit in the light of the moon for a minute or two. It can be inside or out, but should be exposed to moonlight. If you can't see the moon for some reason, put your hands on the top of the container and visualize the full moon's light coming down like a laser to your jar. This is an appeal to your subconscious mind through ritual.
3. While that is going on, if the glycerin settles at the bottom, no worries! That's to be expected. Next, stir or shake (slightly). Start running your bath and pour about ⅛ cup into the bathwater to start and more if desired.
4. You may want to add to the water a fairly large piece or cluster of amethyst, whose frequency admits curative properties and has been used for healing and releasing stress, anger, and anxiety throughout centuries. Literally put it in front of you in the tub, but make sure it's large enough to avoid going down the drain. Also, be sure not to step on it while you're getting out of the bath. If sitting with a gemstone doesn't feel right to you, simply put it on the edge of the tub or counter somewhere you can see it. You could also put it in the tub for a few seconds and remove it. Here are a few other gemstones you could use to help you relax if you don't have amethyst:
   - **Aventurine**: Releases life's daily troubles
   - **Black tourmaline**: Dispels negativity
   - **Rhodonite**: Calms fear and alleviates panic attacks
   - **Rose quartz**: Opens your heart
5. While soaking and indulging in self-love, think calming, uplifting thoughts. Think about what you have and positive future ventures. Hang a picture or painting in your bathroom that represents those things so you can look at it while you soak. Use a visual to get your mind started for a future venture. Or, simply, just be.

Throw a Dinner Party

The full moon is the time to pull out all the stops, gather your friends, and throw a delicious—but at least partially healthy—dinner party. Let all of your energy come together for a feast to sustain you through the next twenty-eight days! Break out your best place settings and pour heart-healthy red wine for your guests. Serve up oysters on the half-shell for appetizers and organically fed chicken breast with grilled veggies for your main course. Dessert can be a decadent experience with a delicious chocolate cake. You'll need:

$1^2/_3$ cups unbleached white flour

$3/_4$ cup date or granulated sugar

$1/_4$ cup cocoa powder

1 teaspoon baking soda

$1/_2$ teaspoon kosher salt

1 cup water

$1/_2$ cup canola oil

1 teaspoon cider vinegar

1 teaspoon vanilla

---

1. Preheat oven to 350°F.
2. Coat a 9" × 13" rectangular pan with nonstick spray.
3. In a large bowl, stir together flour, date sugar, cocoa, baking soda, and salt.
4. In a separate bowl combine water, oil, vinegar, and vanilla.
5. Slowly stir the oil mixture into the flour mixture.
6. Pour into prepared pan and bake 20–25 minutes, until a toothpick inserted at the center of the cake comes out clean. Cool completely.

Don't forget to take time to honor the full moon during your festivities. Perhaps you want to offer a toast to the lunar energy before dinner or while you're waiting for dessert. Gather your friends in a circle and thank the moon for its inspiration, its light, and its continued influence on our lives. As it begins to fade from view in the coming days, the memories of your party will keep you feeling motivated and full of hope until the moon shines bright again.

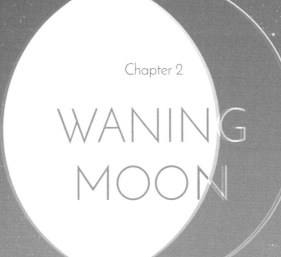

Chapter 2

WANING
MOON

When the light of the moon slowly appears to be getting smaller and smaller, it is a time of surrendering to the power of ending, the power to destroy what is stagnant and decayed. It is a time of tidying up, reorganizing, editing, sifting, gleaning, refining, sweeping away, and clearing space. All things must end to fulfill their beginnings. Sometimes we must create a void so it can be filled, whether with new goals, friends, or relationships.

The waning moon is like a lunar gift that allows you to let go of emotions that no longer serve you. Letting go of emotions also opens the door to forgiveness, whether for others or yourself. Forgiveness can be more effortless when you have the waning moon to help you make that shift from blame or self-pity to tolerance and compassion. Do not overschedule yourself during this phase—be sure to rest more, and allow yourself time to reflect and tune into the feelings of the surrender and release.

Everyone talks so much about new beginnings, but before you can begin anew, you have to discard old unhealthy habits, people who challenge your peace of mind, and places you don't feel comfortable in anymore. Use the exercises in this section to clear out physical, emotional, and spiritual clutter so you are ready for new challenges and successes.

Stop Rushing and Slow Down

It sounds so simple when people tell you to slow down and relax. Of course, you know you should…but you can't today (or tomorrow, or the next day) because you have all these obligations, right? If that's the case, schedule your relaxing time on the waning moon phase. It's moving with the flow of nature, not against it.

Often, we help everyone else but forget about ourselves. As a result, we can end up overworked and under-rested. Even if you can't take a full day off, you can still find pockets of time and space for yourself.

If you are able to schedule some relaxing time, try not to worry about how you'll fill it. You can just be. Find a chair somewhere away from it all and just sit. Use your senses to take in what's happening around you, the smells and sights and sounds. If it might help you, imagine the stresses in your life releasing and separating from you.

Here are a few ideas for relaxing that take 5 minutes or less:

- Have a cup of green or chamomile tea for their stress-relieving properties. (Just preparing the tea itself is a relaxing ritual!)
- Hug your pet or someone you are fond of or love.
- Listen to a relaxing song.

- Eat a banana (which contains lots of potassium and magnesium…nature's muscle relaxers).
- Head outside for a short walk.
- Eat a small piece of dark chocolate with at least 70 percent cocoa content. It's an anxiety reducer.
- Unplug from your devices and take a technology break.

When the moon wanes, its light gets smaller and smaller in the sky. Let your tension follow suit. Visualize the moon above, even if it's morning. Think about how even our lunar buddy takes a break from her waxing and fullness. She takes time to rest and rejuvenate before shining bright again. Be sure you do the same.

Journal and Freewrite to Let Go

When the moon is starting to become less visible and have less of a pull on us, you can start to release some energy and enter a quieter state of mind. Think of letting go of nervous thoughts that haven't been serving you and behaviors that may have been harmful to you in the past. This is a time to find peace and to focus on being centered. One way to help achieve that goal is to start a journal. A waning moon journal can pose questions like:

- Are there energies from the full moon phase that I can begin to let go of now?
- What can I do in my day-to-day life to help me release pent-up emotions?
- What is my spiritual or energetic goal during this phase of the moon?
- How will I know when I achieve my waning moon goal?

Think about writing in the light of the waning moon. Granted, this may not be an easy task for various reasons, but give it a shot. If this isn't going to work for you, try sitting on a lighted porch, deck, or patio, or even sitting by your window inside.

You can also try freewriting for 10-15 minutes in order to get rid of anything that might be blocking your train of thought during traditional journaling or writing. This is sort of like free association in that you keep your pen moving continuously during the exercise. If you feel like you have nothing to say in your writing, then you write, "I feel as though I have nothing to say," and continue on along that tangent until inspiration about another topic strikes.

The waning moon is a time to freewrite about decreasing things that you don't want in your life anymore. Think about what you want to decrease and how you can try to do that in small, simple ways. The most important thing about freewriting is not to judge yourself or to set limits on yourself. The sky (or moon) is the limit!

Minimize the Influence of Toxic People in Your Life

Energy vampires are people who drain your energy. Unfortunately, sometimes the people closest to you are the worst offenders: family, friends, coworkers, and neighbors. The waning moon is a magical time to rid yourself of these toxic influences. You already know who they are—they complain nonstop, argue about anything, or make you feel guilty. For example, they might say something like, "I would have been here on time, but I had to pick up all the things you didn't have time to gather up last week for the charity gala. But no problem. I didn't mind." These people can become very tiresome. It makes them feel better after complaining, but it can leave you feeling like you just went through a storm. Ever hear your phone ring or get a text and think, "Oh, no, it's her again"? What about when you see that car in your work parking lot and your heart sinks? Do you smile all day long when a certain person *doesn't* come to work? Do these people intentionally drag you down? Usually not.

It's easy to say, *Well, just avoid those people!*…but that's not easy to do in real life. However, help is on the way. Protect yourself from them by paying attention to your energy and how it's being used.

Here is one technique you can try:

1. On the night of the waning moon, when the sky is dark and things are typically much calmer, sit down on a chair or lie down if you prefer. If you meditate, get into an altered state of consciousness. If not, just relax.

2. Visualize the person whose energy doesn't sync with yours getting literally getting smaller and smaller, like the waning moon's light. (Of course, the moon doesn't really get smaller, it just appears that way.) Don't wish anyone harm or visualize anyone in an unsafe situation. Just see them diminishing until *poof*, they're gone.

3. Do this for three nights in a row as the moon wanes. You will become aware that the person is now not as dominant of a force in your life.

Another thing to consider is whether you are focusing a lot on people you don't really like. You give them power of sorts by shifting your energy toward the things you *don't* like about them. You are better off putting an emphasis on what you *like* about them. For example, your neighbor might be a nice person, but when he starts ranting about politics, you shiver. If that's the case, when you think about him, think about his love of plants and how nice he keeps his yard. If there is someone who is a drain and you can't find anything good about them…try not to think of them at all. Maybe they won't show up at that party, or they will decide to move to another state. It's amazing the influence you have when you sync your desire to decrease something with the waning moon phase.

Invite Kali or Ganesha to Help Clear Away Negativity

Remember that the waning moon phase is a time to think about what needs to be removed or decreased in your life. This is something to keep in mind during your daily activities—for example, do you *really* need to take a call from a person who's been a lousy friend and who routinely calls only to ask for favors? Some of us have trouble saying no and sticking to our guns, however, and that's where a meditative practice invoking specific Hindu deity energy can buttress your intent.

We are so lucky to live on a planet with a fascinating array of religious and spiritual beliefs. Even if you are not fully immersed in a particular religious or spiritual practice, it's okay to try some of its practices as long as you honor and respect its origins and intentions. For example, you might use Kali, the Hindu goddess associated with destroying evil forces, during the waning moon to help clean out the spiritual cobwebs and detritus left over from old relationships, situations, and life in general.

Kali has also been called the Divine Mother and Mother of the Universe. Depending on which stories you read, Kali is also noted to be a bit of a provoker, but in a good way. She reminds us of our fierce nature and that we shouldn't take a lot of garbage from anyone. In this way, she encourages you to fight back when someone is using you or hurting you. She is most often portrayed in imagery as having four arms and holding a sword, a severed head, a trident, and a skull bowl to catch the blood from the head. Would *you* want to mess with her?

Ganesha, meanwhile, is the elephant-headed deity who is known as the remover of obstacles. Ganesha is particularly helpful when someone is embarking on a new phase in their life—which, on balance, indicates that they are leaving behind or removing something else, whether it's a job, a relationship, old habits, or whatever the case may be.

You can call on both deities in your meditation and ask them to help guide you and sustain you in your new endeavors while leaving your old ways in the past. Here's how:

1. Prepare your meditative space.
2. Set your intention. What type of strength will you need from Kali? What kind of barriers stand in your way that Ganesha can assist with?
3. Now, invoke the deities with a simple request, such as:

   - Kali, I ask that you remind me of my power to state what I want in every situation.
   - Ganesha, help me to move past feeling as though I have to please others all the time.

Offer up thanks to the deities after making your requests, and remember to call on them as needed—they don't mind!

Make Your Own Skin Exfoliant with Sugar

Exfoliating is the process of removing dead skin cells. And what better time to release old cells than the day or night of a waning moon? Make a batch in advance, use it during this phase, and prepare to be amazed by the results! Since the energy of this moon phase is to reduce, get rid of, and make a pathway for a new start, your skin works with that energy to free you of the old so you can renew.

In the spirit of keeping things simple, let's start with a formula that has only two ingredients. **Note**: Always test a skincare product before fully using it. Some people put a patch on their inner elbow and see their reaction after 24 hours.

Waning Moon Sugar Scrub

3 teaspoons brown sugar (you can use fine white sugar as well)

1 tablespoon extra-virgin olive oil (use extra virgin as it's lighter weight)

1. Pour the olive oil in a medium-sized bowl.
2. Slowly add the brown sugar and stir until it forms a paste.
3. Apply to your face or body as needed.
4. As you gently scrub, imagine all those lifeless skin cells making the transition down the drain to exfoliating heaven. Rinse off.

Transfer any remaining scrub into a glass jar and store in a cool, dry location. It should last about two months.

The following recipe has a couple more ingredients, but it is worth the effort and is really fun.

Cumin Sugar Scrub

⅛ cup extra-virgin olive oil

8 drops essential oil(s) of your choice (optional)

1 tablespoon cumin (which has inflammation-fighting antioxidants, repairs skin damage, is antibacterial, and protects from blemishes)

¼ cup white sugar (organic is best)

---

1. Pour the olive oil in a medium-sized bowl. If you are using essential oils, add them now.
2. Add the cumin and sugar. Mix well using a wooden spoon or spatula.
3. Apply to your face or body and then wash off. You will feel how soft your skin is.

You're done! Transfer any remaining paste into a glass jar and store in a cool, dry location. It should last about two months.

If you are mixing the scrub now under a waning moon, and will use it later (during any other moon phase), think of the power you are injecting into the formula. Imagine the waning moon scrub being charged to drop off that unwanted skin the next time you use it. In other words, you can mix at the waning moon with intention and use at any phase. But if you mix and use during a waning moon, it is all that much more enhanced.

Heal Your Skin
with Salt Water

History tells us that more wars were fought over salt than gold, and I can see why. When I think of salt, I use the acronym *PEP*: It preserves, enhances, and protects. Salt can also shield us by soaking up that wave of spiritual doubt we sometimes create.

Your spiritual self can get disoriented if you bombard it with so many negative thoughts, material pursuits, and doubts. Those harmful vibrations can take on a strong momentum. If those negative vibes keep snowballing, they eventually get stuck and make you feel sluggish and down. Salt can cut through that energy sludge, clearing your mind and spirit.

If you are fortunate to be around saltwater, such as the ocean, take a plunge (or at least put your feet in) during the waning moon to purify not only your feet but your spirit. When you're in the water, imagine the unpleasant things in life being washed away. If you don't have an ocean nearby, sitting near a water feature or an aquarium in your home can be helpful. (And no, don't put your feet in the aquarium with the piranha!) Fountains, waves, and filters remind us that water is always moving, and we should not be dormant but flow with life's changes.

Beyond visiting the water, try this saltwater remedy and prepare for a renewal of spiritual pursuits. Salt absorbs negativity and the waning moon gets rid of it. Hence, this moon phase is perfect for a saltwater purification ritual. You will counteract the dark and prepare for the spiritual light to reenter your life. Things you will need:

A container or bucket that holds water,
in which your feet will fit side by side without touching
(some people use a clean plastic wastepaper basket)

2 tablespoons salt

A towel

1. Fill your container with warm water. (You can use any temperature, but warm tends to be more soothing.)
2. Add the salt.
3. Sit in a chair or someplace comfortable. Place your feet in the container. Do not let your feet touch each other or you are reinfecting yourself, so to speak.
4. Let your feet soak for a minimum of 10 minutes. Appeal to your higher power that you return to your spiritual self and don't get off track in pursuing your higher purpose on this planet.
5. When complete, flush the water down the toilet or throw it outside. Clean your container.

Do this ritual every waning moon phase if you feel it's necessary.

Try a Dry Brush Massage to Detox

What do you think of first when someone says they need to detox their body? With the exception of an addiction problem, you probably think of blended drinks, special diets, teas, and solutions that release toxins. Here's another idea: brush away toxins. Dry brushing is just what is sounds like—using a soft, dry brush on different areas of your body. This process cleanses you from the outside in. Dr. Sara Gottfried, author of *The Hormone Cure*, says on the lifestyle blog Blog.DaveAsprey.com that your sluggish lymphatic system is to blame for a buildup of toxins. The lymphatic system relies on muscle motion to improve circulation. If you don't move those muscles, "your lymph can stagnate and waste accumulates," she says. Dry brushing can come to the rescue because it:

- Stimulates the lymphatic system
- Exfoliates your skin
- Unblocks pores and leaves your skin more youthful
- Frees ingrown hairs
- Improves blood flow
- Makes your skin glow

Ready to begin? All you need is one natural-bristle brush. Please don't use your old hairbrush that you always thought was too soft. Buy a new one. They can be found in stores or online (some sites call them body brushes) and usually cost about $10 and up. If you can get one with a long handle, all the better so you can reach your back. If you have sensitive skin or any skin wounds, be careful and seek advice from a medical professional before doing this process.

1. Be sure your skin is clean and dry. Gently brush your feet and work upward. Use long, gentle, smooth strokes. You're not scrubbing a frying pan!
2. Certain areas of your body are more sensitive than others, so adjust pressure as needed.
3. When you finally get to your back, you can use downward motions.
4. Take a rinsing shower after you finish and apply the skin moisturizer of your choice on your skin.
5. To clean your dry brush, put it in a bowl of warm water with a little baby shampoo, swirl it around, and let air dry. Some people also spray or briefly give it a swish in tea tree solution and water. (Be mindful not to leave a wooden-handled brush in the water for too long.)

During a waning moon, can you detox and glow at the same time!

Eat Cleansing Foods

When the moon is becoming less and less visible to us, it's time to focus on anything that you want to eliminate from your life—and this can include parts of your diet that might not be serving your body. Many of us consume foods that our bodies were never intended to process. We're also bombarded with environmental pollutants and chemicals in everything from cosmetics to medications. The liver, kidneys, lymph system, lungs, skin, and colon are detoxifying systems that work diligently to rid our bodies of foreign compounds. And while they do a fantastic job without us ever giving them a second thought, you can help them work even more efficiently!

Think about adding some of these ultra-cleansing foods to help support your body's purification systems during the time of the waning moon:

- **Dandelion root:** Helps with liver and gallbladder function, which are key for healthy digestion. It may also help with skin and eye conditions and support healthy kidney and colon function. This is often sold as tea, and is easy to prepare.
- **Bitter greens:** Kale, arugula, mustard greens, and dandelion greens help support liver function. Add these greens to a salad and voila—instant detox!
- **Bone broth:** Helps to support the immune system and also helps with digestive function. Also helpful with liver detox.

- **Seaweed**: Helps to support the immune (lymph) system and detoxes the kidneys. You can find dried sheets of seaweed in health-food stores and use them to make simple rice wraps. You can also try a fresh seaweed salad for a tangy treat!
- **Turmeric**: An ancient Indian spice that helps with fat digestion. Curcumin, a substance found in turmeric, is a natural anti-inflammatory and antibacterial agent and has been used to treat irritable bowel conditions, joint pain, lung issues, and skin conditions—you name it! You can add turmeric to a smoothie or work it into your dinner plans by adding it to your marinades, sauces, and roasted veggies.
- **Water**: Plain old water helps to keep your body running like clockwork. Water helps to eliminate toxins through the kidneys, keeps your lungs hydrated, your skin supple (to prevent breakdown where bacteria can enter the blood), supports your digestive and elimination system (including your liver and colon), and keeps your lymph system flowing. Aim to drink eight (8-ounce) glasses a day. Add lemon, lime, cucumber, or berries for flavor and additional nutrients!

Try adding some of these detoxifiers daily for the two weeks around the waning moon. Keep a journal noting how you're feeling each day, and then review as the new moon approaches. Do you have any chronic issues (digestive, skin, pain, etc.) that seem to have improved? How about your immune system—were you able to steer clear of a virus that made your entire office sick? Most importantly, take note of whether you found it easy to add these elements into your diet—you might just want to keep them around for good!

Indulge In Soothing Baths and Masks

The waning moon is a time for relaxing, breathing easy, and releasing impurities from your life and body. A great way to achieve these goals is to climb into a detoxifying bath. We've long known that simple Epsom salts can draw bacteria and toxins from the body during a soak. Let's talk about some other bath additives that will help to ease your soul and cleanse your being.

- **Helichrysum:** A relative of the daisy, the oil of this flower has antimicrobial, anti-inflammatory, and antiaging properties. Add several drops to your bath to fight infection, soothe rashes, and boost your skin's radiance.
- **Peppermint:** Traditionally used for nausea and intestinal issues, peppermint can also be added to your bath to soothe skin irritations. The menthol in peppermint is also good for sinus issues and headaches and will be released in the steam from your bath.
- **Rosemary:** This is a good choice for connecting you to the earth while also giving you a calm energy and mental clarity. It can also help to ward off anxiety and fatigue.

- **Neem**: This is a type of evergreen that is native to India. It is said to have antibacterial, anti-inflammatory, antifungal, antiviral, and anticarcinogenic properties.
- **Red clover**: You see this plant all over the place in the summer. Its oil is used typically to calm skin conditions like eczema, burns, and psoriasis.

You can combine a couple of these oils in one bath, but resist the urge to throw them all in at once. You want to give each oil a chance to work its magic on its own.

Beyond baths, you can try other relaxing and calming treatments during a waning moon. Maybe you've have heard about the healing properties of a mud bath, which can soothe skin issues, draw out impurities, exfoliate, and relieve sore muscles and joints. You can actually make your own mud bath by adding moor mud (available wherever you buy your beauty products) to a hot bath. For the ultimate soothing bath, add some of your essential oils as well.

A charcoal mask is a simpler version of a mud bath that will leave your face feeling as good as new! Again, you can purchase a mask wherever you buy your other beauty products. The charcoal helps to draw out impurities and toxins, helps minimize breakouts, and overall gives you a nice, deep cleaning. Use these treatments as a way to focus on your health and well-being during this moon phase.

Release Stress with Breathwork

We meet people in the most unusual ways under a waning moon as we let go, which leads us to an unclouded pathway to start another journey. As I was writing this book, I was selling my house (letting go), and I met someone who came through the door with an overall radiant glow. I thought immediately that she appeared to be healthy, happy, and grounded. And sure enough, she was a yoga instructor, Kim Kruysman, who had been practicing yoga and meditation for twenty years. We discussed practicing yoga under a waning moon. She suggests the following breathing exercise and meditation during the waning moon. (Do not practice this breath work if you have asthma, high or low blood pressure, or respiratory issues.)

Moon Breath or Chandra Bhedana

1. Sit with your legs crossed or in any comfortable seated position.
2. Your left nostril is associated with the moon and its cooling energy, so you will be breathing through the left nostril to connect with this calming energy. Close off your right nostril with your right thumb.

3. Slowly inhale through the left nostril. Pause at the top for 2 or 3 seconds. Place your index finger over your left nostril and release your thumb from the right nostril as you slowly exhale through the right nostril.

4. Place your thumb back over your right nostril as you slowly inhale again through the left nostril. Repeat the sequence for a few minutes.

Now that you are relaxed and calm, you can try the following meditation.

Letting Go Meditation

1. Sit comfortably and rest your hands in your lap or on your knees palms up or down. The first step in letting go is illuminating and bringing awareness to what it is that you need to release. Be open to the illumination from the moon. Close your eyes and bring your attention to what you need to release: pain, anxiety, tension, negative emotions, or anything else that is not serving you. This short meditation will help you to illuminate and let go. Do you have expectations of people or situations that might be leading to sadness, disappointment, depression, or stress? Prepare to release these negative emotions or anything else that is holding you back from experiencing a calm, peaceful, and happy inner self.

2. The mantra for this meditation and practice today is: "I allow myself to open, illuminate, release, and let go." Imagine a small spacecraft. Place anything that you need to release and let go of into this spacecraft: your worries, fears, struggles, grudges, toxic relationships, limiting thoughts, expectations, and anything else that increases negativity and stress.

3. Now imagine yourself pushing a button and the spacecraft lifts up into space. As you watch it slowly disappear, repeat "I release and let go."
4. Now deepen your breath, wiggle your fingers, and bring your awareness back into your body. Slowly open your eyes with a gentle gaze.

Kruysman also suggests a Waning Moon yoga sequence. Try to practice it outside or on the beach, if possible, where you can be illuminated by the glow and energy of the moon. Keep in mind that the waning moon rises after sunset, so you may have to start this practice a little later in the evening. The waning moon is a reminder to invite stillness and a slower pace into life. Set an intention for this slow and gentle practice to open up, allow the light in, and release or let go of what is no longer serving you. Kim states, "May the energy and illumination of the waning moon help you to carry the healthy, positive thoughts throughout your days and remind you to eradicate and let go of negative thoughts and emotions that do not serve you."

Rid Your Home of Old and Stale Energy

If your home has some negative energy in it for one reason or another, take advantage of the cleansing waning moon period and get rid of that vibe. Purchase a natural broom to sweep, sweep, sweep away that dust, dirt, grime, and guess what—old and not-so-old energy!

Witches are often portrayed with brooms in pop culture for various reasons (true or not), but there are tangible reasons that this tool is used in modern self-care rituals as well. Sometimes called a besom, a witch's broom is usually made of natural materials and is used to cleanse an area before performing a ritual or spell there. Besoms can also protect a home if placed upside down near a doorway. Even if you're not a practicing witch, you can use a broom made of natural materials to clear your home of negative energy.

Sweep your natural broom toward the west (where the sun sets and where you should get rid of things). Remember, you are not sweeping literal dust. It's all etheric. If a broom is not available, simply use your outstretched arm and make a swishing gesture. As you sweep, say to yourself or out loud: "Bad energy gone, away away. Good energy come, today today."

You can even just say a few words, such as: "I remove this bad energy."

"Bad energy gone, away away. Good energy come, today today."

Clean Out Clutter

Release and let go is the mantra of the waning moon. We want to release bad habits, people we don't want in our lives, and that extra 10 pounds we put on over the winter. But what about letting go of tangible things—those old tools in the shed and all that fat-free gravy you bought by accident? The waning moon has no preference what you liberate; it's just energy that makes the freeing easier.

Think about a space in your home that needs a thorough decluttering and aim to tackle the project during a waning moon. It's usually not a one-day chore, so allow for a couple. Here are some tips:

- Be organized and collect three bins—one for items to donate, one to throw out or recycle, and one to keep.
- If you run across some sentimental items, ask yourself if you will really miss those items if you got rid of them.
- Play music while you do it or talk on speakerphone to your favorite friend. It doesn't require much thought, so you can have a distraction.
- Be sure to shred any paper items that contain personal information.
- If you have anything worth selling, consider holding a garage sale or posting an ad on a reputable website to sell certain items.

As you make your decisions, put the items in the appropriate bin, and before you know it, you will have opened up space in your home.

This is really a rewarding experience as you are donating to charity, cleaning up, *and* moving forward. You are freeing yourself of old energy that no longer serves you.

Detoxify Your Skin with a Coconut Oil and Salt Scrub

Pamper yourself with this detoxifying scrub to rejuvenate your skin—or present this gift of indulgence to a loved one. Since you will be making it yourself, it's also filled with love. Invoke the powers of your creative self and brew a batch of purifying coconut oil and salt scrub. You'll need:

1 cup coarse salt (sea salt is a good choice)

$\frac{1}{4}$ cup coconut oil

$\frac{1}{4}$ cup vitamin E oil

3–4 drops peppermint oil (or your favorite essential oil)

1. Blend ingredients together and put them in a glass jar with a lid. Think about the person who is receiving this contribution to better their skin as you mix.
2. Gently rub the scrub onto your body and wash off.

Note: Coconut oil will become solid when it gets cold. That does not affect its original purpose. If that's the case, simply place the jar in a bowl of warm water (do not microwave it) to return it to a liquid state.

Here are some fun ways of presenting the jar if giving it as a gift:

- Tie a ribbon around the jar—use any type that makes you think of the recipient, whether it be camouflage, flowered, or striped.
- Include the dates of the waning moon for the year in which you present the gift.
- Include a tiny wooden spoon or body scrubby sponge.

You can include the following instructions (feel free to tweak them to make it more personal):

1. This coconut oil and salt scrub for your body and feet was made with love and the following ingredients: coarse salt, coconut oil, vitamin E oil, and peppermint oil (or fill in the essential oil you used).
2. Use it to detoxify your skin and rejuvenate your day. It's best used when the moon is waning, as a waning moon assists you in the release of negativity in your life and body.

When you are done with your waning moon scrub and free of all that negative energy you encounter every day, it's time to think about what good you want to come into your life when the moon starts to wax.

Give Your Problems to a Higher Power

As the moon wanes, let that phase take your negativity with it! Have you ever felt that no matter how hard you try to switch your thoughts about a bad event or people who did you wrong, sometimes you just can't? At first you may try to be understanding, then you might try to rationalize by thinking something good will come from this. You try other methods, but nothing works and your frustration builds till you're always on edge. Friends tell you to just let it go. You think about it, you try…and then you want to punch someone anyway! Does it make you bad? No. It makes a regular, emotional human being.

In a perfect world, you could thank the person who upset you and tell them how they have given you a better understanding of the words *patience* and *understanding*. But realistically, sometimes the better option is to take your anger and let something else deal with it. I say *something* else as you don't give it to a person; you give it to a nonphysical source. You may say God, Goddess, Source, or Universe. You fill in what you call your higher power.

The best time to make this handover is during a waning moon because you can think of your tribulations getting smaller too. Here is a quick exercise.

1. Picture yourself putting your concern in a big bag, like a laundry bag or Santa's bag. Tie it with a bright bow and hand it to your higher power.

2. Say something like, "Here you go! I can't deal with this anymore. I release my concern and understand it is not something I can resolve by myself. I will cooperate with the solution my higher power is bringing about through me and through others. I am secure in knowing this is being resolved."

3. Finally, recite an affirmation: "I release it to my higher power." This should bring you some peace of mind. If your thoughts keep wandering back to your problem or problems, repeat the affirmation when you start to worry. You might add the word *continue*, as in: "I *continue* to release it to my higher power."

Although I do believe we create our own reality, sometimes on the road to creating we need help, so don't be afraid to ask. Sometimes we have to put things in the hands of professionals, like the team who cut down the dead tree in your yard or the plumber who fixed that leaky faucet. Same thing here. Put your woes in the hands of your source, who knows exactly what to do. Every time you think about it, stop yourself and try to remember that it's in the hands of something else now. You may be surprised at the outcomes of this big bag method.

Practice Forgiveness of Yourself and Others

Forgiveness is a way of letting go emotionally—releasing old hurts, judgments, mistakes, and missteps. Whether the person in question is you or someone else, it's equally important to try to forgive. Holding onto blame and anger hurts you and the other person. The waning moon can make the process simpler, since its energies are focused on decreasing and releasing. Here are some ways to forgive:

- **EFT (emotional freedom technique)** is one way to forgive. Some people refer to it as psychological acupressure. EFT is also referred to as tapping, and it boasts the physiological benefits of Chinese acupuncture without the needles. The goal is to tap on meridians, which are channels of energy present throughout your body. EFT is done by speaking aloud as you tap in different areas, such as below your eyes, the top of your head, and so on. This process can bring your issues to the surface so they can be acknowledged and re-leased. If you're interested in EFT, search in your local area for a certified practitioner.
- Consider **reciting a mantra or affirmation**, which is a phrase or word repeated with intention. On the day of the waning moon, say, "Everything happens for higher purpose." Repeat this 10–40 times per day starting at a waning moon

for two weeks and see if your mood shifts so that you can start accepting a situation that has been weighing heavy on your mind.

- Last, there is a **Hawaiian Ho'oponopono** ceremony. It is a forgiveness tradition that is centuries old but still used today. This healing method provides a special time to make peace with old issues and finally move on. It typically begins with prayer or special words by a facilitator. After the prayer, the facilitator states the problem and the participants talk about their feelings. It is akin to getting pain off their chests. The beauty of it is, no one blames the other and each person takes responsibility for their part in this situation. Everyone forgives and starts new. If you're interested in Ho'oponopono, search online for trained facilitators in your area.

Give yourself and others the gift of forgiveness—it is so freeing to your mind, body, and spirit.

Carry Selenite
to Clear Stuck Energy

Selenite is your go-to moon stone. It's gypsum, which is a mineral that comes in a variety of crystal shapes and forms. You can find it everywhere, on each continent. The colors vary, but its properties include inducing calmness, promoting healing and balance, and providing protection. It relieves anxiety, and during a waning moon, you want to release anything you don't want, especially anxiety and stress. In Greek mythology, Selene was believed to be the moon itself. She was love and light. They thought this moon goddess would travel the sky in a chariot to protect those in darkness.

Selenite mimics the moon, as it reflects white light into any location where it is placed. It has a high-frequency energy and is valuable for spiritual work and meditation.

Selenite works well as a women's talisman and supports her through the changing cycles of her life. Those who wear it as jewelry may attract love, fertility, and remain calm throughout pregnancy.

During a waning moon, place small pieces of selenite in corners of your house or room, as it protects from outside influences. If you have a child who is afraid of the dark, give them a piece of selenite to put on their dresser, desk, or shelf and tell them that the rays of the moon are captured within the stone and shines on them with protection as they sleep. If you are on the shy or timid side, this crystal can remove that feeling of inhibition and improve your social skills. Selenite can also unblock your energy field and support your physical structure. Connecting with it can even aid you in becoming more flexible in your logic and overcome jealousy and doubt.

Selenite is calming and can connect you to source energy if you have been blocked. Incorporate this stone into your meditations or your calls to spirit guides or angels. Simply holding it or having it in view when you are meditating brings forth its influence. Selenite will always deliver.

Make Ayurvedic Spice Mixes to Detox

Our bodies sometimes mimic the moon cycles. When the moon is waning and appears it is reducing and depleting, so can our body, minds, and spirits.

It is a good idea to make meals that are easy to digest during a waning moon so it will form a habit we can keep going beyond this moon phase. Restaurant and fast food can really cause chaos in your digestive system and interrupts its natural flow. If you're also under stress, your body can really suffer from aches, pains, and imbalances.

This is where ayurvedic principles can help. Ayurvedic is comprised of two words: *Ayur*, meaning "life," and *veda*, meaning "science or knowledge." Hence, the meaning is "science of life." Ayurveda is a holistic approach that treats disease and promotes continued good health. It is an entire way of life, so I cannot describe it fully in a few paragraphs, but you can experiment with a few of its techniques and see if it is something you want to pursue more fully.

Following is an Ayurvedic spice blend that promotes healing and detoxing—it's a great choice for the waning moon phase. Spices are very beneficial, and they are fun to work with. This blend contains some spice powerhouses:

- **Turmeric** is an antioxidant and improves circulation. It has been used in India for cooking and healing for thousands of years.

- **Cumin** is an aromatic member of the parsley family. According to a 2017 article published in the *International Journal of Molecular Sciences*, cumin seeds were proven to have anti-inflammatory and antiseptic properties. Weight loss, fighting infection, and aiding digestion are also benefits of this plant.
- **Coriander** is also known as cilantro. The leaves and stem are cilantro and the seeds coriander. This spice helps lower blood sugar. And according to a 2000 study in the *Journal of Ethnopharmacology*, coriander exhibited protective values against colon cancer.
- The **fennel** plant, associated with longevity and strength, is high in nutrients, such as vitamin C, calcium, magnesium, potassium, and manganese. Studies have shown that fennel may benefit your mental health, get rid of a gassy stomach, and relieve heartburn.

Note: Although not a part of the actual spice mix, you'll need ghee for this recipe. Ghee is best described as a form of clarified butter associated with Indian and Southeast Asian cooking. It has many health benefits that butter does not have, such as being anti-inflammatory and anticarcinogenic. Its high-level smoke point allows for cooking at higher temperatures with no damage to the fat. Ghee can be found at most whole-health-food stores and now is fairly available at larger grocery stores.

SPICE MIX
1 part turmeric
2 parts ground cumin
3 parts ground coriander
4 parts ground fennel

OTHER INGREDIENTS
Ghee
Salt and pepper, to taste
Chopped vegetables

1. Mix spices together in a bowl and transfer to a glass jar or small tin. The tin allows for less exposure to light. (You can store the remainder in a cool, dark, dry place for up to six months. The spices will last longer, but their aroma and pungency can become depleted.)
2. Put a small amount of ghee in a frying pan and turn the heat to medium.
3. Add 1 teaspoon spice mix per veggie serving to the pan.
4. Stir the spices till you can smell their aroma. If you like, add salt and pepper to taste.
5. Add vegetables and sauté for 5 minutes or so, depending on the amount you are preparing and your preference.

This spice mix is another way to remove impurities from your body during the waning moon.

Align Your Chakras to Let Go of Negative Energy

The word *chakra* (pronounced *chack-ra*) means "wheel or disk" in Sanskrit, the language of ancient India. A chakra is a spinning energy that is not visible to the eye. Usually, they are depicted in a drawing as seven separate wheels of light located close to the spine. They vary in color from red to violet. Think of chakras as energy centers. Each one serves a different purpose, such as your heart chakra, which is your fourth chakra counting from the bottom of the spine up, and is associated with the color green. Its actual location is not where your heart is but in the center of your chest. It is associated with nature, love, and relationships. When your heart chakra is blocked, you may experience problems relating to others or finding meaningful relationships. Another example is the sixth chakra (the brow or third eye chakra), associated with the color indigo (deep blue-violet). It is the space between your eyebrows and is your center of intuition and insight. When it is out of alignment, you may become moody or have difficult times making a decision. Being out of alignment or blocked affects you mentally, physically, and spiritually. Sometimes, anxiety, fear, guilt, or depression can diminish the movement of these energy fields. Therefore, we must unblock our flow of energy or chakras and get back to being balanced and vibrant.

Negative energy can be a challenge to dismiss. That's why we use the waning moon phase for this exercise. To unblock your chakra and align it properly, you could call upon the help of an energy healer. If you are looking for a local energy healer, look online for recommendations or ask at a new age store, vitamin store, or even a chiropractor. You can also visit an acupuncturist to align your chakras as well. If you do choose to seek an energy healer, make your appointment for the day of the waning moon and you will respond better to the healing.

If you would like to try it yourself, follow these steps:

1. Find a chakra chart online so you can learn what color corresponds with which chakra.

2. Sit in a quiet space in a chair, or you can lie down. Begin with your root chakra, which is associated with red and located at the base of your spine. It corresponds to self-preservation, sex drive, and physical drive. Close your eyes and visualize red at your root chakra.

3. Now open your eyes and consult the chart to find the second chakra. Close your eyes and visualize that color (which is orange).

4. Continue till you have gone up to the top or last chakra.

5. Once you have finished each chakra, visualize yourself and all your chakras in a cloud of white light for a few seconds. End with a final statement, such as, "And so it is," or "Thank you."

Breathe deeply and notice if you feel like your energy has become unblocked and freer.

Cleanse Your Aura

In the earlier Read Your Own Aura with a Mirror entry, I addressed how to read your own aura. Now let's give that aura a psychic scrub. Some people can emanate so much negativity from their aura that others around them will start to absorb it. Whether you're emitting negativity or absorbing it, it's important to cleanse it. Auric cleaning can energize and clear blockages that may restrict the flow of your energy. Once it is cleared, you may feel some relief from depression, fear, low self-esteem, and anything else that may weaken your aura. It raises the vibration level of your auric field, which will break down negative blockage.

If you prefer to have a professional do this, you can hire a Reiki practitioner. *Reiki* means "universal life force energy." Reiki is a method of channeling energy to someone with the intention of healing. A treatment consists of a trained practitioner placing their hands on or near the client's body to direct the flow of energy and unblock areas that need attention.

You can cleanse your own aura as well. First, determine if your aura needs repair so you know your starting point and can see your progress after the cleanse. Read your aura using the process described in the Read Your Own Aura with a Mirror entry in Chapter 1. Is your aura really small? Is it black or really dark? If so, it needs a cleanse. If you're not sure, think of it as preventive maintenance and cleanse it anyway.

1. Sit in a chair where you won't be disturbed. Keep your feet flat on the ground. If the chair has arms, rest them with your palms up in a "receive" position. If not, put your arms, palms up, on your knees.
2. Do not cross anything like hands, legs, or arms—those positions will block the flow of energy.
3. Close your eyes and count up slowly from one to eight. (Eight is a power number according to numerology.)
4. As you count, visualize your body being filled with healing green or blue light. Green is the basic healing color, while blue has healing properties but includes a calming and peaceful effect. Judge what suits you best by using your intuition.
5. See the color entering your toes, ankles, up your legs, past your hips, across your chest, along your shoulders and arms, through your neck, and to the very top of your head and even a little out from there. You are filled with healing light. Relax and feel the purification of light and energy.
6. When you are ready, reverse the procedure and see it expel out of the body the same way in which it entered.
7. Count down from eight and see your body filled with clear light. Say aloud, "My aura is cleansed."

The waning moon will help push that stale energy out of your body and make your effort near effortless. That's one of the powerful perks about this phase.

Recite Chants to Let Go

The waning moon is a time to focus on the things that aren't working in your life, and to think about the energy, situations, and people that need to be cleared out. As the moon's glow—and its pull—starts to lessen and move into a restful period, your soul can follow suit. To help you define your spiritual clean-out list, you may want to try chanting.

Chanting is an ancient practice used to help people focus on their intentions. You can use these phrases during a meditation session or repeat them while you're taking a walk, cleaning the house, or otherwise have some time to work peace, calm, and purpose into your day. Some of the Buddhist chants that will work well for this purpose include:

- *Om ami dews hrih:* This chant invokes strength to help you clear hurdles and obstacles on the way to your peace. If you know you have to get through a tough conversation or will go through a rough patch by cleaning out your friends, a job, finances, or any number of other things, this chant will help bring harmony and blessings.
- *Om tare tuttare ture soha:* This is another chant to help overcome hurdles, but it reminds you not to become attached to one particular outcome and to remember there are blessings coming to you no matter what happens.

- *Tayata om bekanze bekanze maha bekanze radza samudgate soha:* This is a long one! Letting go of old wounds is a painful process. This phrase is an appeal to mitigate that spiritual distress when you're on the path to a new future. This can also apply to physical illness.
- *Om tare tuttare ture mama ayuh punya jnana pustim kuru soha:* This is a chant used when your intent is growth, compassion, and a long and healthy future. It's also used when you're wishing these things for someone else.

Keep in mind when you're moving away from old relationships that you can wish the person well and show compassion for them while still keeping your own best interests at heart. Honoring yourself and your own needs involves saying goodbye to guilt! The waning moon phase certainly is a time to do that; it will support you.

Chapter 3

DARK
MOON

During this lunar phase, you can't see the moon at all. But its energy will surround you and draw to you answers you've been seeking. Some use the terms *dark moon* and *new moon* interchangeably. I always separate the two, however, as I feel the energy is different. I think of the dark moon as a phase until that tiny crescent is in view. Then, I will proclaim the new moon has awakened and a new phase has arrived. The phrase dark moon does not mean dark energy! It merely denotes quiet, tranquility, peace, and contemplation.

The energy from the dark moon is that of contraction, deepening, and a hibernation of sorts—of getting away from the hustle and bustle to connect to something darker and dreamier. It is the time to absorb everything experienced, learned, and gained from the previous moon cycle. It is where the real growth occurs. Though it is the shortest phase, it is still very powerful.

The dark moon phase is similar to the final pose of every yoga class—Savasana, also known as corpse pose, where you lie still on your back for several minutes. This is when your exercise and your practice settles into your body, your soul, and your spirit. Without this pose, you're not able to absorb the full power of your yoga practice. The dark moon is the Savasana of the moon cycle.

Meditate to Receive Messages

The dark moon is a particularly powerful time to meditate because you can gain information from your higher power. (You might identify with God, the Goddess, or Universal Life Force Energy. It doesn't matter as long as you make a connection with whomever it is you think is the source.) I call it the "talk to me" phase because you're likely to receive messages from a higher power.

On the day or night of the dark moon, find an inside location where you feel relaxed. Play music, light candles, have a cup of tea or even a small glass of wine—in short, unwind before you begin the meditation.

1. Sit in a chair or lie on the floor, in your bed, or on a sofa. If on a chair, put your feet flat on the ground. If you're lying on a surface, you should be on your back, straight.

2. Put the palms of your hands by your side, facing up in a receiving position. If you are sitting, you can rest them on your legs or thighs.

3. Concentrate on your breathing. Think, "Breathe in, breathe out." Keep doing that until you can visualize your body engulfed in white light energy.

4. Unlike some meditative states where you may ask for some guidance or want something, during this meditation, you won't start with you; you'll start with your higher power. As him/her/it this question: "What's on your mind?" By asking your higher power or source energy this question, it gives your question a unique jolt, because so few people start a prayer or meditation that way.

5. Continue to breathe in and out until you feel you are getting a thought in your mind that you can decipher. For example, you might start thinking about your career. What does that mean to you? Your higher power is sending you bits of thought that you have to decode. (Of course, it's much easier if you just got a text or a phone call, but it doesn't work that way.) You must do a little work to interpret what pops up in your mind.

6. At this point, you can start to ask questions. Only ask a few or you will get confused. For example, think: "I am thinking of moving in with a friend. Is this a good idea?" Breathe in, breathe out, and see what thoughts come to mind.

When you feel you are finished, give thanks, relax, and wait to see what happens. Remain calm and dwell in the serenity of the dark moon.

Summon Your Angels

Often, individuals who say they are not religious but are spiritual believe in the presence of angels. Texts such as the Bible, Torah, and others address the creation of angels, and many of us have experienced a connection with one at some point. But many of the ancient texts tell us that angels cannot intervene with humans unless we give them permission, as we have free will. The dark moon phase is a magical time for an angelic connection because everything is slow and quiet. The following ritual will help you summon angels to help you.

1. On the day or night of a dark moon, sit or lie on your bed, sofa, or floor.
2. Visualize yourself being surrounded by angels in a circle around you. They may be around your bed, around your chair, or around wherever you are located. Do not give them names or assume it is any of your favorite angels. Just imagine angels in a circle.
3. Try to look closer now. Are they holding hands? Do they even have hands? Do you just see light or some type of figure you can't make out? We all visualize angels differently. Do they have wings or are wings just an artist's interpretation of angels in ancient paintings so they could differentiate between the humans and the angels?
4. Feel the angels' presence, feel their emotion. The important thing is you *feel*. You can even feel sad, if that's what your experience is.

5. Say to yourself (*not* out loud), "I give you permission to commune with me and to help me." Make up your own words if you prefer. You might just say, "It's okay to talk to me and to help me." Thank the angels—always show gratitude for their presence.

6. Ask the angels for what you need to have released, what is bothering you, and if they will assist you. Go into detail if you like, but they will know one way or the other. The key is to give them permission to help you.

7. When you feel you have said what you have to say…wait to see if you get an immediate answer. If you don't, end with a closing statement, such as "Amen," "Thank you," "I love you," or even, "I am so grateful." In the next few days, see if you start to get little signs or hints that help is on the way.

Angel energy works well at any time, but your concentration is heightened at the dark moon as you are more calm.

Take an Herbal Healing Bath

This therapeutic bathing method is truly a lunar luxury. With the moon is in its dark phase, you should relax, restore, and recoup your serenity. It's a perfect time to enhance your bathing experience by relaxing your body, mind, and spirit.

Not only do baths relax you, but you can experience other benefits (such as antibacterial and antidepressant) if you add essential oils to the water. Start by finding the right essential oils or flowers for you. Essential oils are the volatile oils from plants that give them their fragrance. Different types of essential oils benefit us in different ways—one of these might be right for your dark moon bath:

- **Relaxation**: Lavender, Roman chamomile, geranium, sandalwood, and ylang-ylang
- **Uplifting**: Grapefruit, orange, lemongrass, and peppermint
- **Healing for aches and pains**: Lavender, marjoram, eucalyptus, and rosemary

You can also research other essential oils so you can find one or more that match your preferences and needs. If you'd rather have a visual and an aroma, consider using fresh flower petals in your bath. Here are some options:

- **Roses:** Rose petals not only give you a feeling of self-love and luxury, but rosewater also soothes irritated skin.
- **Gardenias:** These are soothing for PMS and stress. If gardenias remind you of Grandma and you don't want to particularly think about her in your lavish bath, choose another one.
- **Frangipanis:** These are a tropical flower (often, Hawaiian leis are made from frangipani). It is associated with love. In the Polynesian culture, a woman may place a frangipani over her right ear if she is seeking a relationship. If it's on the left, she's already taken.
- **Daisies:** Though not really fragrant, they look sweet in the water.
- **Fresh bouquets:** If you have a bouquet of flowers you bought or someone gifted you, let them do double duty. When they look like they have seen better days, toss them in the water and revive them for one last lunar awakening.
- **Dried flowers:** In feng shui, dried flowers can remind us of things fading and going away, but when you add water, they plump up and *presto* they are rejuvenated to happy healers.

If a fragrance or a flower reminds you of something that makes you woeful, don't use it. Encompass yourself by things you find delightful and unique to who you are.

When it's time to relax and relieve your body and mind from tension, turn to this essential oil bath ritual.

---

3 cups Epsom salt

3–12 drops of your favorite essential oils (do not add more than $\frac{1}{4}$ ounce—these oils are powerful) OR

2 cups flower petals

$\frac{1}{2}$ cup baking soda (to soften skin)

---

1. Fill the bath with warm water. Add all ingredients to the water.
2. Be a botanical beauty for a while. Keep the rhythm of that dark moon going when you are adding your oils or petals. Just like the dark moon promotes peacefulness—let the flowers be (if using). Don't try to sink them when you first put them in. Gently toss them or place them on top of the water and let them float. Later, you can swish and scoop them around if you like, but at first, allow them to relax as well. Lastly, don't let the flower petals go down the drain. Scoop them out with a strainer or colander before you drain the tub.
3. Light candles for ambient lighting, play relaxing music, and immerse yourself in comfort.

The most important part of this bath is to take the time to honor your well-being.

Carry Gemstones and Crystals for Contemplation

Gemstones and crystals have special properties used for certain times in your life depending on what you are trying to achieve. Following is a list of gemstones geared for use in dark moon applications like meditation, divining, and contemplation. I am sure you will have a preference if you further explore each one.

- **Apache tear** is a type of black obsidian that absorbs negative energy. According to lore, it has the power to heal one from emotional distress and anguish.
- **Black obsidian** is a prevailing cleanser of psychic haze, if you will. It is a protective stone and negates unwanted influences. This is excellent to have on hand if you are doing any kind of prophesy work or are trying to "see" the future.
- "Talk to me" is what **chrysocolla** would say if it could speak. It is a stone of communication. Its very core is that of expression, empowerment, and ideas. Its turquoise-blue color calms you and helps you get in touch with your inner wisdom.
- **Fluorite** is a stone used for grounding your spiritual self. It assists you in increasing your psychic abilities, connecting to life force energy, or becoming one with universal consciousness.

- **Jet.** Don't leave home without it if you are a healer. Jet aids in healing your organs and is especially effective at minimizing migraine headaches. Wear jet when you are grieving or disheartened as it will absorb that undesirable emotion. It's a cleanser for impure energies, especially when the moon is dark and we tend to become more inward in our thoughts and feelings.
- **Labradorite** rings the bell of transformation. It strengthens and preserves. Your psychic abilities are like muscles—the more you work them, the bigger they get. This stone helps you to strengthen that muscle.
- **Rainbow obsidian** gets its name from the fact that when you polish it and expose it to powerful light, it displays the colors of a rainbow. It is the stone of peacemakers and gentle souls. Use this when trying to help others or send them positive and restorative energy.
- **Red jasper** is a calming force. According to some Native American cultures, it symbolizes Earth's blood, making it sacred. It is a stone of the earth and grounds, heals, and mends all aspects of your life.
- **Snow quartz** projects a feminine energy. It's the warm and fuzzy feeling kind of stone. It provides balance and alignment and is helpful for achieving mental clarity and awareness in meditation. It's also beneficial to wear or carry if you are trying to make a relationship decision.
- **Zircon** crystals have a highly spiritual influence. They are all about respect for others and vibrate to a love frequency. They will help you get in touch with your spiritual self.

When you select your favorite (and it's okay to use more than one at a time) you can wear them, carry them, or simply place them in front of you or off to the side for convenience's sake. The connection to the spirit of the dark moon will magnify their properties!

Journal Your Dreams

Carl Jung described the "shadow self" as the part of us that we keep suppressed or that we don't consciously recognize. Most of us live our lives on a "have to" basis. We have responsibilities, deadlines, time frames for achieving goals, and we never stop to think about where we got our ideas about life to begin with! Who says we *have to* have a family or make a specific amount of money or live in a particular kind of home? And is that what you really want or is it just expected and so you go along with developing your life in a certain way without really thinking about it?

Your dreams can answer the deep questions you don't even realize you need to ask. The images and adventures that come to you during your sleeping hours can reveal spiritual gaps that you need to address. The dark moon—with its pitch-black nights and low energy—is a time when many people sleep more soundly, and your dreams can reveal issues you need to resolve during your waking hours.

A lot of people say that they don't dream, but, actually, we all dream. It's a biological process that researchers believe helps to restore the brain and memory and also helps us sort out the day's issues. If you're someone who doesn't remember their dreams, it may help to keep a dreamtime journal. Here's how:

1. Place a small notebook and pen on your nightstand or somewhere you can easily access it from your bed or sleeping area.

2. Place a penlight or small flashlight near your notebook so you can jot down information at any time during the night without turning on a lamp and possibly disrupting the rest of your sleep.

3. Whenever you wake up—during the night or first thing in the morning—take a minute to review your dreams. If you have trouble remembering your dreams, take some deep breaths, keep your eyes closed, and try to remember any fragment of a dream. Often, if you can remember just one small detail, you can follow that thread to recall larger elements of a dream.

4. Sometimes dream elements will come back to you during the day. If that's the case, write them down! If you can, also take a couple of minutes to close your eyes and let the rest of the dream come back to you.

Now, look for patterns. For example, dreams about falling often indicate some kind of worry or anxiety. Flying in your dreams indicates you've overcome an obstacle. When you've identified a few common elements in your dreams, research their meanings. Then use meditation and chanting to work out the issues that have come to light in the darkest phase of the moon.

Try a 24-Hour Fast

There are many religious and spiritual motives to fast, such as giving the god of your understanding more attention through prayer and reflection. Healthwise, fasting gives your body a rest and can be purifying and healing. Whatever reason you choose to fast, it is something to ponder. The onset of the dark moon is an advantageous time to begin a fast, because you can get in rhythm with the lack of moonlight and emptiness in the sky. Since your body will be empty and devoid, you are somewhat mimicking this phase.

If you should decide to do a fast, determine why you are doing it. It is for health reasons? Spiritual reasons? Both? When you fast for religious or spiritual reasons, you are humbling yourself before your higher power. Consequently, prayers may be answered more readily and situations resolved sooner because you are in a better state to allow positive resolutions and requests to come into your life. And if you don't immediately get what you're asking for, you are still in a better state of acceptance and understanding.

If improved health is your goal, fasting comes with many benefits. Some researchers feel it can reduce heart disease risk, decrease bad cholesterol, and help maintain proper body weight. The list is vast and the research extensive. But keep in mind there are cons to fasting, as well. It could cause dizziness, especially if you exercise (therefore, exercise cautiously if you're fasting).

Like anything else directed at your well-being and health, always check with a doctor or medical professional to see if you are a candidate to do a 24-hour fast. Discuss what is best for you. Will you be drinking only water? Will you make it a juice fast? What will you eat when it's time to end your fast? Make your plan in advance.

To help you with detailed questions, ask your doctor and consult some books, such as *The Transformational Power of Fasting* by Stephen Harrod Buhner or *The Complete Guide to Fasting* by Jason Fung and Jimmy Moore.

Do a Past Life Regression

A past life is the theory that we have lived in another lifetime and returned again after our death to a new lifetime. We don't remember the previous life, but we might retain residual fears or talents that we can't really explain. For example, you might hear from the believers (or at least the open-minded people) things such as, "I don't like bridges—I must have fallen off one in a past life."

You can do what's called a past life regression and find out who you were and where you have been and see if it makes sense to you. The suitable choice is the day or night of a dark moon because it is a time for reflection and study. The veil between who you were and how you came back is thinner at this time.

If you prefer, you can find a trained practitioner who will do a past life regression for you in the form of hypnosis or other methods. Some will do a tarot card reading and see a few past lives. (Most of us have had more than one.)

If you are private, you can do it yourself. Here is a quick method where you will pick up at least one past life. Note: Before you start this exercise, be sure to state your preferences. For example, if you do not want to remember or reexperience any past life that is tragic, say, "I do not want to experience anything violent or upsetting." (You can put it in your own words too: "No really negative stuff." The universe knows what you are thinking.)

1. The day or night of a dark moon, get relaxed in a meditative state by sitting in a chair or lying down.
2. Visualize a room with five doors in a semicircle in front of you. You will be walking through these doors as someone you were in a past life.
3. Look around your imaginary room in your mind and choose a door. Breathe in and out a few times, then imagine someone walking through it. That's you from a past life.
4. Is it a man or woman? (You have likely been both.) What time period does their attire reflect? You will sense who you were. Talk to your past life "self" and ask them to tell you what happened. Try only one or two doors in a sitting. If you repeat this again at another dark moon, you can pick the same doors and you may get different results. (Most people have had many past lives.) If a door opens and no one is there, try another. You may be one of the few who is a new soul and have had few past lives.

This experience will give you insights about déjà vu, which is the feeling you have already met someone you are meeting for the first time. Or a place you have never been to that seems so familiar to you. Past life regressions can be very healing as you get answers to things you could not understand before.

Read Someone Else's Aura

At this dark moon phase, the energy is low and you vibrate at a subdued frequency, which makes reading auras easier, as you are not distracted. That said, it's still a good idea to have a meeting set up at a quiet and private place, like your house or apartment. To read another's aura, it best to get a willing volunteer. Do not allow onlookers or other friends in the room. (Too many people can deplete your concentration.) If there is someone else with you, have them go into another room.

1. Have the person sit in a chair with a white background, like a wall, behind them. (Prop up a white sheet or cardboard if you don't have a white wall.) Stare at the middle of the subject's forehead—the third eye.
2. Keep concentrating. Eventually, you will see the area around the person becoming brighter and more in focus than the backdrop actually behind them. You're now seeing their aura. The more you concentrate, the sharper it will be.
3. You never know what you will see. It could be one color or several. (Revisit the Read Your Own Aura with a Mirror entry in Chapter 1 for more information on what certain colors mean.) Typically, the brighter and more intense the aura, the healthier and more spiritually evolved

the person is. The more uniform the aura is, the more balanced and less scattered or confused the person is. The appearances of dark or smoky-looking colors can mean negative overtones, such as depression, ill health, or even unhealthy eating habits. Flashes of colors can mean a person is scattered or not balanced at the time.

Once you get the knack of reading people's auras, you won't have to do it with a white background behind them. You will be able to zone in on anyone and read their aura. However, please don't go around starring at people's foreheads!

You can also read your own aura during a dark moon, then compare it to the reading you did during the full moon. What was the same? What has changed?

Practice Isometrics

Because the moon is not visible during the dark moon phase, we tend to think that its energy is completely absent. This is not entirely true. In fact, what we experience during this time is a sense of peaceful energy. While many of us feel a restlessness and vigor during the full moon, the dark moon comes in with the opposite vibration—a kind of quiet strength that allows you to regenerate.

During this phase, most of us won't feel the urge to run a marathon or lift heavy weights. Those exercises are explosive in nature and don't jibe with the energy of the dark moon. Lighter workouts with isometrics exercises will keep you fit during this time without wearing you out.

Isometrics exercises involve contracting a muscle and holding it in one position (as opposed to isotonic, in which you're contracting and releasing the muscle repeatedly). Don't be lulled into thinking that these are easy moves, though. Isometrics exercises are strength builders, and you'll likely break a sweat simply holding the positions.

Here are a few isometrics exercises to try during the dark moon:

- **Wall sit**: Position yourself about a foot from a wall and lean your back against it. Now lower yourself into a seated position so your thighs are parallel to the floor and hold. Start with 15 seconds and work your way up to 1 minute in 15-second increments.

- **Plank:** Put yourself into a push-up position, with your hands directly under your shoulders. Level your body so that you are straight (like a plank). Make sure your rear end is not sticking up in the air. Aim your hips to the floor. Pull your abdomen in. Hold for 30 seconds and work your way up to 1 minute.
- **Glute bridge:** Lie flat on the floor with your knees bent. Lift your hips and clench your glutes. You should feel this contraction in your hamstrings as well. Your abdomen should be tight, and you'll feel your weight pushing down through your shoulders. Hold for 30 seconds and work up to 1 minute.
- **Boat Pose:** Sit on the floor with your knees bent, arms straight out. Lean back slightly and lift one leg, then the other, by using your abdominal muscles to keep you steady. This one requires balance and strength, so start out with your legs straight in front of you if you need to. Eventually you'll work your way into a *V* shape. Hold for 30 seconds and work up to 1 minute.

Repeat these exercises five times each. You will definitely feel the burn in the morning!

Experience Natural Healing from Walnuts

Walnut is often hailed as one of the best psychic and spiritual boosters you can find. It's said to help with transitions of all kinds, especially when someone is trying to leave negative energy behind and focus on new beginnings. During the dark moon, when we withdraw from high-energy and high-drama situations anyway, we also want to put into practice useful tools that will help us to achieve new goals. Using walnut flower essence is an easy way to start looking forward.

Walnut flower essence comes from the walnuts we are most familiar with (English walnuts) and is sold in bottles, usually with a dropper. You can take the essence by mouth (read the label carefully for dosage instructions), or you can add several dropperfuls to your bath. As you soak, you will bring to mind the situations and relationships that you want to change as the moon starts to come back to us in the coming nights.

Black walnut is a little different than walnut flower and has a bolder, earthier taste than the walnuts most of us usually eat. However, it does have healing properties of its own, most notably as an antioxidant when eaten. Black walnut oil is used as anti-inflammatory, antifungal, and antibacterial agent, which makes it a perfect natural treatment for anyone who has athlete's foot, swelling, or a simple little skin infection that needs some drying out. (Black walnut contains tannins, which are known to pull fluids from tissue. Be aware, however, that tannins are known to cause migraines, so if you are prone to beastly headaches, black walnut is probably not for you, especially in its true nut form.)

This hearty nut has been hailed over the centuries as a cure for everything from cancer to syphilis to simple skin issues. Obviously, your doctor is your best source of information if you have a serious medical issue, but for the less acute conditions, try soaking in a black walnut bath during the dark moon. If you want to keep light out of the room and your eyes, wear an eye mask or a tie a scarf over your eyes in keeping with the spirit of the darkness of this time.

You can also create your own foot bath by removing the hulls from black walnuts and soaking them overnight in a small tub. In the morning, remove the hulls from the water and voila! You're left with your very own all-natural solution. You can even add additional antifungals like crushed garlic. Soak for 30 minutes, then dry. Repeat daily until the problem area shows improvement.

Enjoy Yogic Sleep (Yoga Nidra)

The dark moon, when the moon retreats from us and is invisible to our eyes, is the perfect time to withdraw from the stresses of the world and live rather like an animal in hibernation. Extra sleep time, naps, and meditation can and should be priorities for this phase, as our souls and minds need time to replenish themselves on a regular basis.

One form of deep rest and meditation is called Yoga Nidra. When most people think of yoga, they envision striking and holding poses—and indeed, this is also yoga. Yoga Nidra, however, specifically focuses on achieving a semiconscious state midway between being awake and alert and being fully asleep. This state is called hypnagogia, which is reported to help reduce stress and tension, develop intuition, inspire creativity, and fuel inventive work.

When practicing Yoga Nidra, the goal is to block out every sense except hearing, so that you're in a state of suspended consciousness, only listening to directions for relaxation. The directives are given either by a yogi in a studio setting with others who are also practicing Yoga Nidra, or they may come from a recording. You can get a free app called Insight Timer, which includes many Yoga Nidra meditations and a description of each one. The main difference between this practice and meditation is that in meditation, you remain mostly alert, although you may achieve a state of deep relaxation. In Yoga Nidra, you are almost entering into a sleep state. To prepare for Yoga Nidra at home:

1. Find a spot where you can lie flat and relax comfortably and completely.
2. Consider your intention. What is it you want to achieve during this time? Stress reduction? Connection to your higher self? Improved creativity or thought patterns?
3. Do a body scan to identify any areas of latent tension, areas that you may be clenching or contracting without realizing (like your jaw or shoulders).
4. Start to breathe deeply. Count to eight as you breathe in and then to ten as you breathe out. Let your breath become slow and regulated.
5. Allow your thoughts to come and go freely. Don't judge yourself for intrusive ideas or stressors; rather, just set them aside for now.
6. If you can avoid falling asleep completely, you can continue on this path by yourself. Otherwise, it's best to use a guide to keep you from dropping off into a deeper sleep.

Listen to the guidance from the yogi or your recording and recognize when you start to feel that you're between consciousness and sleep. When you've reached this state, you can observe yourself and your thoughts more easily—all the background noise is gone.

Yoga Nidra can help to decrease stress while increasing room for joy in your life. Practice this during the nights of the dark moon to emerge feeling as fresh as a bear from a cave in the spring.

Weed Your Yard

Just like you should use the dark moon for balance and rest, so should your plants—after all, they are living things. Each moon phase influences the soil on our planet. Our ancestors planted according to the moon phases, and many of us still do. You will see advice about planting according to the lunar phases in most *Farmers' Almanacs*. These resources often state that one of the best times to prune your plants is when the dark moon is in the sky. This stems from the fact that it is believed that the moon governs moisture, and at the dark moon, the moisture is not very elevated. There is little gravitational pull and is more of a dormant period growing-wise so the weeds won't grow back as fast.

Therefore, when the next dark moon occurs, be prepared. If you have a garden, pull some weeds. It's a great form of gentle exercise too! Putting your hands in soil is healing for you as well, since you are getting in touch with nature—something many of us don't do often enough. Many individuals believe that plants and trees have healing energy. Studies are still ongoing about the health benefits you can get from putting your hands in soil, or even just being near trees or plants. Whether you want to literally hug a tree or just relax outdoors in the fresh air, you're likely to feel more relaxed afterward.

If you can't get outside because of the weather, you can instead prune inside plants, like a bonsai tree or kitchen herbs, in a meditative way. No matter where you are, forgetting about daily concerns is easier when you're focusing on nature.

Attempt Remote Viewing in the Shadow of a Dark Moon

Remote viewing is a way of using visualization techniques to view a place, an event, or an object without actually being there. Some people consider it an out-of-body experience, while others find it more like clairvoyance.

You will want to try remote viewing during the dark moon phase, as this is a quiet period, and you need to concentrate so you can be projected to where you want to go in your mind. The best way to get started is to first see if you have a flair for it. To do this beginning stage, you will need to find a friend, as this is a two-person endeavor.

1. On the night of the dark moon, have a friend or someone who will help you with this experiment over.

2. Decide who will be the viewer and who will be the sender. The sender is the person who is going to go somewhere and look at something, and the viewer is a person who is stationary and tries to draw what the sender is looking at. (Note: Being able to draw well or be artistic does not matter at all.) Have a paper and pen or pencil ready. You can be inside or outside. The viewer needs to stay put in one place. (In a group, have one person act as the sender and the others stay in the room and follow the same method and see who is the closest.)

3. The sender should go somewhere else in the house or apartment without telling the viewer where they are going. You can take it one step further and the sender can drive or walk to another location.

4. Once the sender finds a spot, they call the viewer and tell them that they are staring at something and to draw what they are staring at. Give the viewer several minutes to try to see, then return. The sender can write down what they were staring at before telling the viewer, or they could take a picture with their phone.

5. Reunite and see how close you come. For example, if the sender went to the parking lot and was looking at a telephone pole and the viewer drew a straight line... that's a hit. Or maybe the sender goes into the bathroom and looks at the shower curtain with bubbles on it. If the viewer draws a square with round circles...that's a hit. Or even just circles...that's a hit.

This is only one experiment in remote viewing, and the subject can be expounded on if it's something you want to pursue further. Sometimes people claim they are so proficient at this they can find lost people, pets, or see occurrences. If you research a government program called the Stargate Project (not to be confused with the film), you will find more information on the topic. The experiment was cancelled in the 1990s because they never came up with satisfactory conclusions. Whether you think it's possible or not, it's very interesting to see how you do. Some people take this very seriously, while others think of it as a party game or a fun thing to do with friends.

Have Your Fortune Told

The dark moon is an ideal time to have your fortune told. The world is dark and peaceful, so you can concentrate, and the psychic abilities tend to be even stronger.

Whether you are a believer or not, most people are fascinated by fortune telling and psychic abilities. Fortune telling (or intuitive counseling, as it's sometimes called now) dates back to before recorded history. Nearly every culture has its own methods of foretelling events and situations that lie ahead.

Today, many technology advances and logical scientific methods abound, but simple nature still sparks most of us to want to know what the future will bring. To find a professional to read for you, ask around locally for recommendations or suggestions or surf the Internet and see if some of them sport a website that appeals to you. When looking for a reader or any type of intuitive, follow your gut and choose someone who you feel comfortable with.

For the sake of the reader and to get the most bang for your psychic buck…keep an open mind to the experience. If you go to a reader ready to attack or be critical, you should not go at all. There's nothing worse than a client coming in and the reader says, "How are you?" and the clients spouts back, "You should know; you're the psychic!" You have not only made a bad joke, but it also shows that you are challenging them before you even get started.

Be open and embrace the adventure. Relax and see if the quiet of the dark moon can offer you any insight into your future.

Use a Pendulum to Find Answers

A pendulum is a weighted object attached to a string or chain that is used for divination. It is best used for receiving *yes* and *no* answers from your inner self or subconscious mind, helping you to make decisions and to get clarity.

The dark moon phase is excellent for working with a pendulum because the moon's energy is slow and less likely to interfere. (Since it is a form of prophesy, using a pendulum during a full moon also works. Still, I find the dark moon creates an atmosphere of steadiness, calmness, and relaxation, all of which are key to working with pendulums.)

Pendulums already made are the easiest to use, because they are balanced and all set to go. You can even use a necklace with a pendant and chain. Some people use a gemstone such as crystal or amethyst (promotes intuition) as a pendulum because of the vibrations they emit, but any weighty object can be used. You can also easily make your own by attaching a weighted object to a string or chain. Simply get a 6–9-inch piece of string, chain, ribbon, or yarn and a weight for the end: a pendant, pin, heavy earring stone, seashell with a hole, etc. will do. Make sure the weight is fastened in such a way that the knot isn't off to one side. The idea is to make it hang straight.

Once you have your pendulum, you will need a target card that provides a focal point. Use a piece of cardstock or cardboard with a small circle drawn on it—the heavier the paper, the better. Or use something like a coin or button. Anything that acts as a bull's-eye. Wash your hands before you proceed and visualize any energy field of impurities or outside influences that you may have picked up going down the drain of the sink. Then follow these steps:

1. The day or night of the dark moon, sit inside at a table or on the floor—somewhere you are peaceful. If outside, make sure you are in a safe place and consider the wind. Wind moves pendulums! Place your target card or bull's-eye on the surface in front of you.

2. Hold the pendulum suspended from one hand (either one), with the weight approximately 1 inch above the center circle. You can bend your elbow or keep your arm straight. Still the pendulum so it is not moving.

3. After you have steadied the pendulum, you need to determine the directions for *yes* and *no*. These will be different every time. Therefore, do not write the words *yes* or *no* anywhere on the target card. To determine the directions for *yes* and *no*, ask a question silently or out loud that you know the answer to, such as, "Is my name _____?" Then ask a question you know has a *no* answer. The pendulum should swing in the opposite direction of *yes*. If it doesn't, try again until you get clear directions for *yes* and *no*.

4. After you go through this setup procedure, you can ask all the questions you choose. Don't go overboard! If you find that the needle of the pendulum is going in circle or in a direction that makes no sense, stop and start over.

The pendulum is a springboard for tapping into your subconscious to find out what you really want in life.

Try Dark Moon Numerology for Beginners

The dark moon is a time of relaxation and contemplation and a time to learn something new that requires very little studying or effort—like numerology. Numerology is the ancient study of the vibration of numbers and their meanings to interpret your path through life. It's all about adding up numbers and learning the meaning of each number. I will explain the fundamentals in a very simple format, but if you are interested, feel free to delve deeper into the subject.

In essence, you will be adding numbers and reducing them down to one single digit. Each digit from 1 through 9 has a meaning (positive and negative). The exceptions are 11 and 22, which are considered master numbers. People who are master numbers are gifted with exceptional power and potential beyond most people. These people are said to have a high levels of intuition and intelligence. Numbers 33, 44, and so on can sometimes be considered master numbers as they are the pairing of the same number. But that will not be addressed here, and I suggest you do further research if you have one of those numbers.

Let's start with your birth date and reduce it down to one digit. This number can tell you a lot about your life's path and your nature.

Example: Birthdate: January 24, 1990

First, add the numbers together. January is 01 for the first month of the year. Day 24 when added together is 6. Year 1990 when added is together is 19 (1 plus 9, plus 9, plus 0). The total of these numbers equal 26. However, that is not a single digit, so you have to now add 2 plus 6. You would be a number 8, since 2 plus 6 equals 8. Your path of life number is an 8.

You can also take an address and add it down to one digit. For example, 2343 = 2 + 3 + 4 + 3. If you have a unit number in addition to your street address, add it in.

What kind of energy will you find in that space? You can also add phone numbers, hotel room numbers, and so on. Reduce to a single digit, unless you get a 11 or a 22—leave those as two-digit numbers for a simple reading. Once you've got a single digit, look at the meaning of each number and learn more about the person, place, or thing:

1 (One)

- **Personal interpretation:** Individuality; you are a leader but better in your own business
- **General:** Independence, new beginnings, creativity, unconventional
- **Negative aspects:** Aggressive, laziness, self-centeredness

2 (Two)

- **Personal interpretation:** Team player, peacemaker, kind
- **General:** Diplomacy, duality, patience
- **Negative aspects:** Oversensitive, not aggressive

3 (Three)

- **Personal interpretation:** Creative, popular, nature lover
- **General:** Enthusiasm, talent, sexuality
- **Negative aspects:** Jealousy, assumptive

4 (Four)

- **Personal interpretation:** Organized, logical, responsible
- **General:** Leadership, protection, solid
- **Negative aspects:** Stubborn, impatience

5 (Five)

- **Personal interpretation:** Loves freedom and change, excitement seeker
- **General:** Versatility, travel, unconventional
- **Negative aspects:** Not stable, excessive

6 (Six)

- **Personal interpretation:** Creates harmony, artistic, giver, entertainer
- **General:** Beauty, social, accountable
- **Negative aspects:** Too proud, meddling

7 (Seven)

- **Personal interpretation:** Understanding, wise, loner
- **General:** Learning, teaching, meditation
- **Negative aspects:** Lazy, boredom

8 (Eight)

- **Personal interpretation:** Powerful, successful, public speaker
- **General:** Ambition, business, metaphysical
- **Negative aspects:** Strict, overdone

9 (Nine)

- **Personal interpretation:** Achiever, experiences abundance, advice giver
- **General:** Intuitive, serenity, imagination
- **Negative aspects:** Moody, bashful

11 (Eleven)

- **Personal interpretation:** Master number of illumination; they are old souls, function on a higher plane, have vast knowledge, and enlighten others with spiritual advice and leadership; are the inventors, preachers, and psychoanalysts
- **General:** Psychic awareness; they can be an inspiration to humanity
- **Negative aspects:** Aloof, skeptical, can be high strung at times

22 (Twenty-two)

- **Personal interpretation:** Master number of a universal path; they are master builders for humankind and do everything on a grand scale
- **General:** Leadership, visionary, achievement; they are the diplomats, promoters, medical professionals, and scientists
- **Negative aspects:** Anxiety, indiffernce, can be so bright they have to keep their stability in check

Numerology deserves more research if you are intrigued. It can even give you an edge on how you relate to people and situations on a daily basis. Before you know it, you won't be entering a friend's house or planning a trip without doing the numbers.

Honor Yourself
with a Ritual

Every once in awhile, you should think about yourself and how wonderful you are. No, that's not selfish; it's self-care! What better time to celebrate yourself than the quiet, reflective moments of the dark moon?

We are all unique. But how specifically are you unique? Write down what makes you you. Remind yourself of why you are so special and irreplaceable. Allow that dark moon creative process to take over your pen. Leave the screens out of this—only use pen and paper.

Make a list of your favorite attributes, and think about ones you don't like as well. You might be able to think of them in a positive light if you try. For example, you might see your laugh as too loud, but you could also think of how your laugh represents your ability to find joy and humor in life.

Turn your attention to the next dark moon and be inspired by its exclusivity and honor your own self. Here's what to do:

1. Sit in a comfortable spot inside or outside in a safe place.
2. Play your favorite calming music, light candles, and/or burn incense. Create a mood just for you.

3. Get your favorite paper and pen or chose something that you gives you a joyful feeling. For example: If there is just something that you like about your Joe's Automotive Repair pen, use it. Any paper will do as long as you like it. You can write on anything. I write on the back of old envelopes. Why? Because it makes me smile, and I have repurposed as well!

4. Make a list of 3–10 things you like about yourself. Be conceited, be proud, be shallow. It's okay. Give yourself permission to say nice things about you.

5. Take a minute and think (don't write it down) about what you don't like, but how to change it into something upbeat. For example: I am sometimes temperamental, but I am proud I am working on the realization that not everyone thinks like me. I am understanding of that more each day. I am unique, but so are they.

6. Once you have your list composed, recite it out loud while you gaze toward the moon. If you can't see the moon, visualize it. (Note: You can write your list inside and say it outside or vice versa.)

7. When you are done reciting your list of self-admirations, keep your list somewhere special. Keep it till the next dark moon to see if there is anything you want to add or take out.

If you're wondering what wonderful thing you might want to take out after the next lunar cycle, it could be something as simple hair color or a temporary tattoo.

Remember, this exercise is about reminding yourself what you love about you. Celebrate your unique, abundant, magical self!

Perform Shadow Work to Promote Acceptance

The shadow self is a psychological term for everything we can't see in ourselves—often the parts we try to hide and deny. It might include traits that we're ashamed of or embarrassed about, or it may be a side of ourselves that we've just never considered or learned about. These are the very things that keep us limited and prevent us from reaching our highest levels of energy. Productive shadow work leads to authenticity, empowerment, creativity, energy, and personal awakening. To be your most authentic self and to live your fullest life, you need to explore your shadow side, and there is no better time to do this than during the dark moon, a quiet time of peace and tranquility. The dark moon provides a unique opportunity for introspection and inner work.

When you learn more about your hidden thoughts and attitudes, you learn more about others, also. For example, when you realize that some of your judgments are based on fears and old wounds, then you start to understand that this is true for other people, too, and that nothing is personal. For example, if someone is nasty to you for no reason, you can pretty quickly say, "This person must have some pain in their lives to be treating me so badly without cause," instead of taking on their negative energy and getting wound up in it.

Here are some ways to start your shadow work:

- Acknowledge your emotions as they come up, without judgment. We all have a variety of reactions to events. When you experience an emotion that you think is wrong in some way—for example, you're jealous when a friend gets engaged, or you're irritated when someone seems to be acting extra nice—ask yourself why you feel this way. Are you afraid that you'll never find a soul mate or do you think that nice people must be phony? Explore your reasons for feeling this way.
- Consider journaling about those feelings so that you can find the origins of them. Journaling might also help you identify other areas of your life where the shadow self is lurking.
- Meditation is a useful tool for exploring hidden ideas and judgments. Use this time to explore long-held beliefs and challenge them. Ask your higher power for protection and assistance.

This can be a painful process, so practice self-care! Old psychic wounds often prefer to remain hidden, but when you expose them, you start to heal. Be kind to your physical and emotional body. Love yourself and remind yourself that you are a perfect and wondrous creature.

When you shed light on the darkest corners of your mind, it opens up areas of creativity, compassion, empowerment, and energy that can serve you much better than those old wounds ever could.

Set Boundaries to Protect Yourself and Others

This protection ceremony can be done as often as you desire on the night of the dark moon. This a preventive way of keeping opposing forces, people, and situations out of your life. It is best done with two or more people. (Doing this same ceremony on the night of a full moon works too, but in that case, you use the strength of that phase, and in this phase, the dark phase, you use the lack of resistance.)

You will be launching a shield of protection. Plan in advance. The night of the dark moon, everyone involved should be free of other commitments and be ready to shut off their phones and devices. One person should be appointed as the group leader or facilitator. This person is responsible for everything being in order. The ritual is usually done inside (since you can't see the moon anyway). However, if you opt for outside, find a safe and comfortable place. When you are ready, follow these steps:

1. All attending must form a circle. If only two people are participating, face each other. It's okay if some individuals choose to sit in chairs or others opt to sit on the floor or ground. The important thing is that a circle is formed.
2. You may choose to hold hands. If that is the case, everyone should do so, or no one should hold hands at all. The energy will not be completed if some are holding hands and others are not.
3. Once everyone is in place, the facilitator should take his or her spot in the configuration and begin the ceremony. He or she should say,

―――

"Close your eyes. As I count up from one to ten, imagine yourself leaving your physical body and drawing closer to the moon.
One...Breathe in...Breathe out slowly.
Two...Breathe in...Breathe out slowly.
Three...Feel yourself ascending toward the moon, even though you can't see it.
Four...Sense the energy of the moon coming nearer and nearer.
Five...Inhale and exhale slowly.
Six...As you exhale, imagine any negativity that you now carry or feel may be projecting toward you in the future being stopped by a shield of white light.
Seven...Feel the vibration of the moon.
Eight...You are now connected with the moon's positive energy.
Nine...Keep your eyes closed. Absorb the power, the life force. You are part of that source energy, not just an onlooker. Take a moment and just be." (Facilitator should allow 5 to 10 seconds of silence.)
"Ten...Continue to keep your eyes closed, and I will now recite our intention."

―――

1. The facilitator now says, "We are gathered here in this special place to use our cumulative energy to create a force field of light that will not allow any type of negative force to penetrate into any areas of our lives. It will not perforate our health, work, creativity, finances, or emotional states. See around our entire group, who have united here tonight, a solid windshield of light that runs in a circle of protection around everyone in this circle. As we depart from this circle, the circle of light will be taken with each and every one of us."
2. All say together, "And so it is."
3. The facilitator continues, "Now see yourselves coming back to the earth slowly to the place we stared from tonight." (Facilitator must provide a few seconds of silent time.)
4. Then he or she says, "Once you feel again present, open your eyes and relax."
5. The facilitator must then ask, "Are we all back?" After everyone says yes, the facilitator should say, "Now you may leave the circle and relax and reflect on what you just experienced." If people want to stay in the circle and discuss their experience, they can. This would be an appropriate time to enjoy refreshments and socialize.

Perform a Candle Ritual

Since the dark moon is a time of, well, darkness, get ready for the next phase by lifting yourself out of the shadows with a candle ritual. Ask whatever higher being you believe in to help you bring more light into your life. You can even imagine the light coming from inside you, glowing and healing. We all have times we want to step out of the figurative dark, whether it's a minor problem or a major one. You might simply want to be a little more cheerful or get rid of a huge burden that's weighing on you.

I highly recommend you do this inside and out of the wind. However, if you are in a situation where the outdoors will work, that's fine. (Always be safe.) Things you will need:

- A candle (white or off-white to represent cleansing and protection). Any style candle will do: dinner candle, votive candle, candle in a jar, etc. The most important is that you have a place in which to carve. Always put standalone candles like votives or dinner candles in a safe holder.
- A toothpick, pen, or open paper clip (something with which to engrave)
- A lighter or matches
- A cup or candle snuffer (something with which to put out the flame—yes, you can blow the candle out, but it can scatter wax)
- Soothing music or incense (optional)

1. Start your music and light your incense, if using them. Set up all of your items on a table, dresser, or somewhere solid.
2. Write the thing or issue you want to release on your candle. If you don't have space to write very much on your candle, abbreviate. If you can, it's best to carve on the *top* of the candle. If you're using a dinner candle, engrave as close to the top as possible. Example: Want to stop thinking about that ex love? Write his/her initials. Want to get rid of your money problems? You could carve dollar signs. If your wishes are hard to capture in written form, draw an arrow pointing up and just think about what you want vanished.
3. Light your candle. As you light it, see the situation you want to go away, going up to the skies in smoke. Then see a ray of light generating from inside of you and feel the peacefulness. Seal the universal deal by saying ending words like, "And so it is," or "Let this go for good."
4. Now you can extinguish the candle. Tip: If you are blowing out a candle, put your finger, pointing up, in front of the flame and when you blow, the air will blow around it, not scattering wax. Remember, that's in *front* of the flame, not *in* the flame!
5. Safely dispose of the candle in any manner you feel suitable.

The dark moon is the time to calmly contemplate things. You don't have to be totally inactive, though. You can light a candle and think.

Chapter 4

NEW
MOON

The new moon is considered the first phase of the lunar cycle. This is time to ponder the word *launch*. That's what you are doing: launching ideas, actions, and even new ways of life. As the moon's light gets brighter and stronger, so will you.

You don't need to spring into high-intensity action overnight, though. Take the time to do a little here and there with the notion that a slow ramp-up will generate a greater outcome. You are like a bear coming out of hibernation slowly. It is an awakening. It's similar to a new year (January 1), except it happens every month. Keep things simple as you move through this phase.

It's interesting that according to the holistic theories of Ayurveda, the air and ether element, known as vata, is dominant during the new moon, evoking a cool and reflective atmosphere. Take note of that, as you should be cool and calm as well. Simple foods and quiet times are called for too. This is a lovely phase. Use it wisely with the following suggestions.

Meditate to Launch New Ideas and Endeavors

The new moon is a time we can start fresh thoughts and launch new objectives. The following meditation can assist you in initiating those pursuits. Some meditations are meant to have you rest your body, mind, and spirit with no intention of wanting to achieving anything. You are just being. But here, we are looking for an altered state of consciousness where you can use that state to tap into the universal source energy to create something to help you start that passage into a new quest.

Foremost, decide what you want to achieve within the next three months. Keep to this time frame and be realistic. If you don't think it's really possible, neither will your source energy or higher power. Not to mention you just wasted a good moon cycle! Break down bigger goals into smaller chunks so they fit better into this time frame. Then follow these steps:

1. Find a special space where you will not be disturbed. Be inside unless you are in an extremely safe location. Turn off your electronics. Dress comfortably. Be as relaxed as you can. Keep your spine straight. Yes, you can lay down flat, but many people fall asleep laying down. If you are not one of those, go for it.

2. Close your eyes and bring your attention to your breathing. Think to yourself, "Breathe in…breathe out," and keep repeating that. Get a rhythm going. If your mind wanders, and it will, that's okay. Bring your attention back to "Breathe in…breathe out."

3. Eventually, you will find yourself in a deep concentration. This should take about 1 minute. This is when you start to concentrate on what it is you want to achieve. Think about what you want, what it will feel like when you get it. Where will you be? What might you be wearing? What will the weather be like? Who will be around? In other words, be a specific as you can. If you can't go into all that detail, just think about the feeling you will have when you succeed.

4. Continue to do this once a day for three days while the moon is in the new moon period.

5. Then, do your meditation once a week for the next three months, no matter what the moon phase. Start paying attention to little signs that your goal is coming your way. There is no such thing as coincidence. An event like a coworker quitting the job that you want is a definite sign. There are signs all around us.

Walk During
the New Moon

Many of the activities, rituals, or ceremonies in this book can be done inside or outside. This is one of the exceptions. You must be outside if you are going to walk by the light of the new moon.

Walking is good exercise at any time, but under a new moon it also has a thought-provoking quality. We all want to walk under a full moon so we can see her shining face and illumination, but when you walk a *new moon*, it's actually more beneficial and inspiring.

This is not a walking meditation because you don't want to be in the present—you want to focus on the future. It's just walking and thinking. The new moon already has your back and projects that commencement attitude to guide you along life's path. Here's what to do:

1. The day or night of the new moon, pick a location where you can walk alone safely. When you walk, carry your cell phone, iPad, or paper and pen.

2. As you walk, think about your foremost ambition, or maybe two at the most. Do you want to graduate, do you want to travel, start a career, have enough money to move, or get that job? Stop walking and write down that target. Now continue walking and think about what you will have to do to get there. Will you have to first get rid of your debt?

How are you going to do that? Do you have to disconnect from someone in your life who is keeping you back? How are you going to do that? Be specific. The wrong answers are: "I just need to get money. I just need to find a job. I just need to get better credit. I need to look better." You need, you need, but what are you going to create to accomplish this? Right choices: "I will take that job at the market for two months while finishing up courses. Then, I will start applying to here or there. I will tell my girlfriend we need to go our separate ways because…but I wish her well. And I will do it today."

3. Walk some more. The more you walk, the more you stop and make notes or record. Keep in mind, you don't want to walk so far that you can't make it back to where you began. So, if as you walk and see a bench or such, feel free to relax and continue your writing.

By the time you are back to your starting point, you should have a decent plan inspired by the innovation of the new moon.

Care for Dry Skin with Herbal Remedies

The new moon is not just a time for new thoughts and ideas—it's also about launching new routines. So let's get free of irritating chemicals and those unpleasant alcohol-based products that do your skin no good. Try launching a home remedy or two for your dry skin. Since you're doing this with the intention of harnessing the moon's energy, being healthy, and improving your well-being, you will be mentally, spiritually, physically, and creatively tapping into this lunar phase!

Following are some natural remedies for dry skin that a friend of mine who has beautiful skin shared with me.

- **Milk:** Use milk to soothe dry skin by dipping a washcloth in it and applying it to your skin for 5 minutes. Milk's lactic acid is great for soothing dry skin. Lactic acid, which is a form of alpha hydroxy acid (AHA), works to boost collagen without irritating skin. The milk bath goes back thousands of years. Historians tell us Cleopatra bathed in donkey's milk. You can use various types of milk, such as whole cow milk, coconut milk, goat milk, rice milk, or soy milk. Powdered milks are fine as well. Select whole varieties instead of low fat. In the tub, the more milk fat, the more nourishment for the skin. Experiment with different types of milk and see what you like the best. Before you take a milk bath, check with your doctor to see if they are safe for you.

- **Honey**: Honey is one of the best natural moisturizers. It is naturally antibacterial, full of antioxidants, and it is great for slowing down aging. It also is soothing, and creates a glow. As a bonus, honey is clarifying because it opens up pores. Before a bath or shower, rub the honey gently into spots of dry skin and leave for 5 to 10 minutes. Rinse it off when you shower.
- **Oatmeal**: Blend a cup of plain oatmeal into a fine powder using a blender, coffee grinder, or food processor. Instant oatmeal, quick oats, or the slow-cooking type all work. Mix into a warm bath with even distribution. Soak in the bath for 15 to 20 minutes, then rinse and pat yourself dry when you get out.
- **Olive oil**: Mix a spoonful of honey with a spoonful of olive oil and a squeeze of lemon juice (a natural skin brightener). Apply this lotion to dry areas and let sit for 20 minutes. Wipe off with a warm washcloth.
- **Avocado**: Avocados have high concentration of vitamin A, which is great for your skin. The honey adds moisture and opens your pores. Make a simple face mask using half of a ripe avocado and ¼ cup honey. Mix the avocado and honey together in a bowl. Apply to your face. Leave on for 10 minutes, then wipe off and rinse your face.

Let the energy of the new moon help you make these soothing treatments a habit!

Choose a New Gemstone

Before or on the day or night of a new moon, go gemstone hunting via a shopping expedition. The new moon will guide you to the vibrational match with your new gemstone. It's much better to buy gemstones in person, where you can touch the stones. If not, in advance of the new moon, you will have to do your best online and hope the person who chose the gemstone for you had a feeling they should pick a certain one for your order. When you are selecting stones, remember that you want to harmonize with them so you have better body, mind, and spirit alignment. Here are a few options for common issues:

- **Azurite:** Application, mental development, insight.
- **Carnelian:** Motivation. Confidence. Breaking through things that may be blocking your creative self.
- **Clear quartz crystal:** Balances the elements and is the most useful gemstone for psychic endeavors.
- **Malachite:** Protects and negates fear. Good for travel.
- **Moonstone:** Femininity, starting anew, destiny. Assists you in unlocking the moon's energy.
- **Snowflake obsidian:** Gives you hope in times of despair.
- **Turquoise:** Healing, good health, revival. Unity with Mother Earth.
- **Yellow sapphire:** Creates success and manifestation of things you want in life.

Clear your new gemstones under the new moon by putting them on a white cloth or piece of paper where the moon could see them if she had eyes. As you set them out (inside or outside) on your white cloth or paper, close your eyes for a moment and see the light of the moon coming down on those stones. The moon won't be bright, but visualize it like a flashlight beam...very directed at your stones. Do this for only a few seconds. Your gemstones are now cleansed and charged for a new round of use.

If you can, try to have at least ten gemstones. Put them somewhere you can spread them out.

Every day, look at your stones and pick them up and touch them. Which one feels the best in your hand for that day? If in jewelry form, wear it. If it's just the stone, carry it with you for the day. The stone will balance that in which you are depleted. Repeat this ritual every day if you like. There is no limit. Or you may stop doing it when you feel you have a balanced feeling daily and no longer need to carry or wear it. You don't have to pick a new one daily. You can use the same one as the day before if you think you are still drawn to it.

Whatever gemstone you pick, imagine yourself connecting with the new moon and seeing how it will carry you to your aspirations with passion and purity.

Improve Your Workspace with Feng Shui

Feng shui (pronounced "fung shway") is the ancient Chinese art harmonizing your environment and the flow of energy by placing items in certain places. This energy flow is called ch'i. Putting it simply, feng shui takes into account a space's energy and helps you set it up in a way that's beneficial for your spiritual health. By simply moving furniture, mirrors, decorations, etc., you can change the lives of the inhabitants of the space. The new moon gives liftoff to ch'i and boosts and enhances the energy of any area you rearrange using feng shui.

Many interior designers are trained in the art of feng shui and use it as a guiding principle in their designs. Some people who have no training use intuitive feng shui—they know what feels good to them. You can go into great detail with feng shui and put crystals inside walls and lights and mirrors in spots that negate negative energy, but during the new moon, we are going to arrange your desk with color using feng shui. After the dark moon, a time when the darkness gives us rest and contemplation, it's time to introduce some light into the next phase—the new moon phase. This is a time of inviting new ideas. If you are in a creative field, you may need some fresh inspiration. If you are not in a creative field, you may still want your work to go smoothly in an organized way. Introducing color to your desk is like lifting stagnation and procrastination from your work area. Lunar feng shui in the new moon phase is about bringing light and color into dark places. Whether this desk is at your workplace or in your busy kitchen, you can use these ideas to help attract things you want into your life.

Feng shui is based on *bagua* (pronounced "bah-gwah"), which is the octagonal symbol of the *I Ching* (an ancient text of divination that offers guidance). The *I Ching* links nature and humankind to each other. Feng shui builds on that concept to enhance the harmony of a space using ch'i. You can print a full *bagua* off the Internet, or refer to this simplified version for the purposes of this activity. The *bagua* is divided into nine sections as shown:

Purple: Wealth and money	Red: Fame, rank, or reputation	Pink: Marriage, relationships, and partnerships
Green: Family, unity, and bonding	Yellow: Mental and physical health	White: Children, or if you don't have children, creativity, or both
Blue: Knowledge, learning, and spiritual growth	Black: Career, promotion, and job	Gray: Helpful people, and can also mean travel and assistance

Those colors mentioned enhance what you want from that area. For example, if you want more wealth, you would put something purple in the upper left-hand corner of your desk. It could be a stone like amethyst or just a purple statue of a poodle. If you wanted more people to help you, you might put something gray in the helpful people area, such as a notepad with gray paper. Most likely you may have a computer monitor in the middle of your desk, which is your health area. You can attach a yellow smiley face sticker or anything yellow to it, as that is the color for good health in the *bagua*. Rearrange your workspace using these colors and locations as a guide, and see if you have any positive changes.

Perform a Random Act of Kindness

The new moon is all about fresh starts. This is a special time to think about doing something kind for someone else. You can do this anytime, of course. But, by timing it, you are more likely to get it done. If it makes someone smile, improves their lives, or gives them hope… you have helped. Whether you give your time, money, or resources to others, you'll be improving their lives, and yours too!

Once, I experienced this domino effect firsthand. It was the night of a new moon. I was standing in line with my husband going to a charity event for disabled veterans. Music, food, comedy…that kind of thing. The line was long and the July heat in Florida, even at 6 p.m., was challenging. It was a slow process getting through the door. So we all proceeded at a snail's pace up the walkway toward the entrance.

The man in front of us was a veteran. He was alone, walked with a cane, and looked happy. The people in line were starting to look anxious, hot, sweaty, and some were complaining about disorganization and so forth. To say the least, the energy of the group was going downhill. At one of our delays, a man put a chair out for this veteran. The vet thanked him and sat down. The man who offered the chair just turned around and started talking to his friends. He may have thought that although it was a nice thing to do, that chair wasn't going to change anything much but give someone a place to rest for a few minutes on the journey to air-conditioning.

Suddenly, when a woman saw this kindness, she decided to offer water not only to this veteran but to others, as she had several bottles with her. Then a man with a harmonica started playing and people started laughing and clapping. There was a total energy shift, thanks to that one act of kindness that snowballed. You may have seen a version of this in your own life—when someone does something nice for you, you're more likely to do something nice for someone else. Start this chain reaction yourself during the new moon.

Make a Vegan Sandwich

On a new moon, you should be starting fresh. If you've been considering a new diet or lifestyle, try it for a day (or even for just one meal!) at this adventurous lunar cycle.

Some people plant on the day of the new moon, as gravity pulls water up, causing seeds to swell, burst, and grow. With all that inspiration, why not try a recipe with sprouted bread, as a tribute to sprouting and the new moon. Sprouted-grain bread is also healthy because it retains more of the nutrients. It is made from sprouted wheat kernels that have been ground and baked into the bread. There are many variations on the market, so read labels and ingredients to find the one that suits you. Some of the breads (such as Ezekiel) are found in the refrigerator section because they have no preservatives. If you're an advanced lunar sprouter, you could make your own, but let's travel the path of least resistance first.

This sprouted bread vegan sandwich is filling, nutritious, and easy to put together for a quick lunch. You'll need:

2 slices sprouted-grain bread (try toasting it)

2 teaspoons any flavor hummus

3 slices avocado

3 slices red onion

3 slices tomato

3 pieces any flavor lettuce

Salt and pepper to taste
(or you can skip it altogether if the hummus has kick)

1. Spread both pieces of bread with 2 teaspoons hummus.
2. Sprinkle the hummus with a dash of salt and a dash of pepper.
3. Assemble the sandwich with the avocado, onions, tomatoes, and lettuce on top.

Serve the sandwich with veggie chips on the side if you like. Various kinds of veggie chips can be found at most grocery stores and at whole food stores. This lunch is easy, healthy, and so new moon!

Smudge and Bless Your Home

Clearing energy from people, places, and things is a really effective way to start something anew. If you don't, it's like taking a shower and putting back on dirty clothes. What's smudging, you ask?

Throughout history, many cultures have burned herbs for ritual and spiritual practices to purify, restore, or cleanse the energy of places. Smudging is also used to purify the body, mind, and spirit. Basically, with the sweep of these burning herbs, you are removing toxic or old energy from former residents. You are removing negative vibes from a person who is in a bad emotional space or removing adverse feelings from an object.

If you have an herb garden with lavender, sage, rosemary, or sweet grass, you can make your own smudge sticks. If you are blessed to have these herbs, once the herbs are dried, bundle a bunch of them by layering each stem and trimming to level the end of the stems. Wrap the bottom of the bundle with a cotton string in a crisscross manner, making sure the bundle is tight and no leaves are billowing over. If you don't have an herb garden, you can purchase sage or rosemary bundles at some specialty garden stores or online. (If you want to mix the herbs, just dismantle the bundles and reassemble them mixed together.)

Safety first: Make sure that the space you are smudging has windows or some other means for smoke ventilation. If you are smudging a person or thing, go outside, and that solves that requirement. Do not use smudge sticks near infants, pets (especially birds), or individuals with sensitive respiratory systems. Like a fire, never leave burning smudge sticks unattended.

Perform your smudging ritual during the day. The light will help burn away the negative energies with the smoke. To smudge, you will need:

A smudge stick

A firesafe container to safely extinguish the smudge stick (some people use giant seashells or a decorative ashtray)

Sand, soil, or salt

---

1. To begin the smudging ceremony, light the smudge stick and blow on it to see it smolder. Keep the extinguishing container under the smudge stick at all times to catch any ash that may fall. If you are having problems keeping it lit, occasionally blow on it to keep the embers burning. You want smoke, not fire!
2. If you are smudging a space, such as a house, simply walk through the house, and in a circular motion, move your smudge stick and visualize all negativity leaving up and out with the smoke.
3. If you are smudging an object or a person, walk around them outside and do the same thing.
4. Write your own blessing in your own words, or you can use this one: "May this space be blessed with peace and safety through the energies of our creator." (You can fill in with God, Goddess, Source, whomever, or just use creator.) Or really keep it simple and say "God, (or whomever) bless this space."
5. Extinguish the smudge stick by putting it out in the firesafe container.

When you're done, the space, person, or object you have smudged will be free of previous energies or attachments.

Cocreate with the Energy of a New Moon

The new moon is a time of increasing and building energy. With each passing day, the lunar pull becomes stronger, calling on you to respond with your highest intentions. This is a phase of creation, to be sure—and if you cocreate with another person during this time, it's twice as powerful. You can expect fireworks when two spirits set an intention together and revel in the possibilities of this phase! It's pure fun and absolute joy.

Find a friend (or two) whose energy matches your own and who will be open to the idea of playing with the universe. The two of you might want to think about an art project, or redecorating one of your homes, or trying out a new skill like photography or a joint writing project. Maybe the two of you want to start a communal garden during this time or start hiking or exploring nature in other ways. The whole idea is to begin something that's new and to enjoy the process.

To set an intention for cocreation with a friend:

1. Sit quietly together and join hands.
2. Take ten deep breaths together.
3. One of you can take the lead in speaking your joint intention out loud.
4. Give yourselves a minute or two to sit in silence, hands still joined, to allow your energies to merge.
5. Try not to get hung up on specific results at this time— focus on the process.

You can also work with your four-legged pals to establish new routines. Start taking your dog for a walk every morning, or introduce him to a new toy or game. (You may not be able to teach an old dog new tricks, but he might enjoy playing fetch.) You may want to introduce a new treat during this phase, or even look into making treats from scratch at home! To set an intention with your animal:

1. Choose a time when your pet is restful. Sit quietly and place a hand on a spot that's comfortable for them.
2. Close your eyes and envision your ideal outcome for this being.
3. Ask the universe to help you work with your pet's energy toward reaching this goal.

Maybe neither of these options sound like your spiritual cup of tea. If that's the case, cocreate with your higher power by using meditation, chants, or journaling.

Journal and Freewrite to Plan Your Future

The new moon brings about a period of rebirth that's yours to embrace. Think about it—every month you have the opportunity to merge with a brand-new energy and use it for your highest purpose! This is a time to focus on fresh starts, setting the loftiest goals, and following your intuition.

Journaling and freewriting are perfect ways to define your goals and monitor your follow-through from month to month. Most people are already familiar with how to journal. During this new moon, you might want to add a little extra zing to your written pages. For example:

- Cut pictures from magazines that help you define your aspirations and paste them into your journal.
- Break out the colored pencils, glitter, stickers, or whatever adds life to your written word!

Freewriting can be added to your journal, or it can be a separate activity altogether. The idea with freewriting is to set structure and inhibitions aside and just let what's in your mind flow out onto paper. You can start with a theme of sorts, or you can simply let the words come to you. Here's how to set up your new moon freewriting time:

1. Prepare yourself with plenty of blank pages. This activity is meant to cover a lot of writing ground, so to speak, and you want to make sure that you don't hit a roadblock by running out of paper.

2. Set an intention for this time. If your intention is simply to write without stopping, that's good enough, because the new moon is a time of creativity. Other intentions might focus on new relationships, career changes, new living spaces, or any new and positive change.

3. Start writing and keep your pen moving! Even if you need to write about feeling stuck with nothing to say, keep writing until other thoughts move in to take their place.

4. When you're finished, go back and find the parts of your freewriting that are useful. These ideas can be used as a springboard for more structured journaling.

5. Don't feel bad if most of what you've written seems useless. The whole point of freewriting is to let your ideas come to light—some will be productive and others won't be.

This is usually a timed activity, so shoot for no more than 15 minutes at a time. If it helps, you can create a ceremony around your freewriting to open up your mind and reach the deepest recesses of your imagination. Take a relaxing shower, light a candle, and meditate for 15 minutes prior to writing. You may be surprised by the thoughts that come up for new moon exploration!

Take a Mud Bath

Many health spas now offer mud baths and maybe even a massage to go with it. If you have a special event coming up, or just want to pamper yourself under a new moon, seek out spas that offer mud baths. Mud baths are natural stress relievers, and unless you go with a friend (which is a great option too), it also gives you some alone time.

Mud baths offer many health benefits, such as:

- Removing flaky and dry skin
- Eliminating muscle tension and joint pain
- Improving circulation

Take a gamble and remember, if you haven't done it before, the new moon is a great time to try something new. Maybe you'll end up making it a new moon tradition!

I love do-it-yourself undertakings, but making your own mud bath can be a bit tricky and problematic for plumbing, so I think you should leave it to the professionals. Instead of taking your time to mix your own mud, use the Internet or make calls to see who in your area offers a mud treatment for the entire body. If not, you can get a mud facial—but dunking your whole body into an entire tub of mud and feeling the warmth, the relief, and the luxury of Gaia (in Greek mythology, Gaia was feminine and the representation of Mother Earth) is a special experience.

Check with your medical professional to make sure you in are in acceptable physical condition for undertaking mud bath. You want to be sure you're hydrated before you go in, so drink lots of water beforehand. Before you visit a spa, don't be afraid to ask questions! Tell them about any health concerns and ask what to do and what to expect.

If you don't want to go muddy, go mustardy. That's right, mustard is not only for bratwurst and hamburgers. You can bathe in it to open your pores, draw out impurities, and stimulate sweat glands. It's like eating hot peppers! You'll sweat out impurities. This is a traditional English therapeutic remedy for aches, pains, colds, and fevers. A recipe for a standard mustard bath is as follows:

$\frac{1}{2}$ cup baking soda

2 tablespoons powdered mustard

2 drops rosemary essential oil

2 drops eucalyptus essential oil

---

1. Mix together all ingredients and pour into a clean vessel. Start running your bath and add $\frac{1}{4}$ cup of the mixture under running water.
2. Relax in the water for up to 30 minutes. Don't be surprised when you really feel the heat from the dry mustard! The essential oils will mask the smell of the mustard, but not the heat.
3. After you bathe, stay warm until your pores are closed. Drink water before and afterward to stay hydrated.

If you don't want to make your own mixture, look for Dr. Singa's Mustard Bath, which you can buy online and in many pharmacies and wellness stores. Or, find a spa that offers mustard baths to its clients.

Start the new moon with a rejuvenated body and spirit. Plus, you have taken the step to try new (green) avenues of well-being and contentment.

Drink Herbal Tea

The new moon signals the rebirth of the lunar cycle when the moon comes out of the hiding phase of the dark moon and begins its journey across the heavens once again. To welcome our lunar friend back into the fold, why not host a tea ceremony?

A traditional Japanese tea ceremony, which is what most of us envision when we think of this ritual, is given with several purposes in mind: to welcome and show respect to a guest and as a means of establishing a deeper relationship with the guest. Simultaneously, the ceremony is almost a form of moving meditation, as harmony and tranquility—between host and guest, and between participants and the universe—are the ultimate goals. The Japanese tea ceremony is truly a thing of beauty, both spiritually and aesthetically. Its hand movements are very specific and learned over a long period of time. If you are interested in learning more about the meanings behind the choreography of the ceremony, ask a librarian for some books about the topic. It's simply stunning and yet very powerful in its grace and simplicity.

You can host a less formal ceremony that borrows some of the traditional elements but is manageable for a beginner. The ceremony will help you welcome the moon to its new cycle, honor its energy and divinity, and seek serenity not only during the ceremony but for the following twenty-seven days. Some things to think about including in your ceremony:

- **A tea set.** Think about purchasing a tea set at a consignment shop, or bring out those fancy tea cups that you never use—this is a special occasion!

- **Friends.** Include a small group of like-minded, harmonious individuals.
- **A group intention.** Make this an important part of your gathering. Sit quietly as a group, join hands, close your eyes, and set an intention for the month ahead.

Matcha (which means "tea" in Chinese) is served in the traditional Japanese ceremony, but because we're not practicing a formal ritual, you can certainly branch out and try other calming teas. Ask your doctor if it's all right for you to try one of these options:

- **Skullcap:** Decreases stress and anxiety, and also helps with insomnia.
- **Catnip:** Our furry friends love this plant because it helps to decrease jitters and support a sense of well-being. It can do the same for you too!
- **Hops:** Helps to increase GABA, a neurotransmitter that relaxes and calms the nerves.
- **Oatstraw:** Used for insomnia and promoting a sense of relaxation.
- **Valerian:** May help to decrease anxiety, insomnia, and even pain, as valerian is a natural muscle relaxant.
- **Ashwagandha:** Used to manage stress, promote a sense of well-being, and lessen anxiety.

There is power in community, so remember to honor the new moon as a group while you relax and welcome the next month with open arms.

Go Green

Most of us want to honor our planet and future generations by choosing eco-friendly foods and materials. But, sometimes going green *costs* a lot of green ($$). The new moon is a pivotal point for forming new habits. Even if you can't afford to go green with the passion you want, you can try your best once a month for a few days when the moon is new. Here are some ideas to get you thinking about getting into the green routine. First, do your shopping responsibly by purchasing earth- and people-friendly items:

- Bring your own shopping bags instead of using plastic.
- Save our beautiful dolphins by buying net-free tuna.
- Opt for chemical-free meats.
- Buy organic milk, cheese, and yogurt.
- Look for certified organic vegetables and fruits.
- Choose earth-friendly cleaners that are plant-based and biodegradable.
- If you use paper-based greeting cards and invitations, choose ones that are made from recycled paper.
- Check out cruelty-free body care products.
- Gardening under a new moon? Use ecological gardening products.

Buying green is a good start, but there are also actions you can take that are simple as well. This new moon can be the onset of changes you make for a new way of life:

- Replace your shower head with a low-flow style. Some use 75 percent less water!
- Instead of using disposable plastic containers for food, use glass jars.
- The bleach has to go! Keep toxins out of the ecosystem, not to mention your body!
- Buy a reusable coffee filter instead of using paper ones.
- Cut down on bottled water by installing a water-filtering system on your sink and using glasses or reusable water bottles.
- Only have a few plants? Collect rainwater and use it to water plants.
- Don't forget about animals in need. Donate your old (clean) pet items to a shelter or pass them on to another needy animal.
- Perform regular maintenance on your vehicle. You will reduce emissions and might not need to purchase a new car.
- Walk, carpool, bike, or use public transportation when you can.
- Get rid of phantom energy use. Many electronics consume energy even if they are not active. Unplug those chargers, microwaves, and computers when you are not using them. It can save you up to 10 percent on your electric bill!
- Lower the heat and use your pets to keep you warm. Try cuddling with your dog when those cold winds blow. That's where the expression "three-dog night" derived!

Let this next new moon be the motivation for going green, if only a few days, or better yet, for a lifetime. You can make a difference in the environment around you, and you will be rewarded with benefits such as fewer toxins and lower bills. It's a win-win.

Color In a Mandala

Coloring isn't just for children—it's a form of peaceful but active meditation. It's highly therapeutic and can quiet your busy mind. Plus, being creative can make you feel productive and fulfilled. Plus, you might get so engrossed in the colors and the activity that you don't have time to think about day-to-day problems. Even medical professionals are convinced that stress can be released by engaging in fine motor movements of the hands. When you have less anxiety, you can focus on big-picture things like planning your future, discovering financial solutions, and taking care of yourself and others.

There are many pictures and designs you can color, but a popular pattern to work with is a mandala. Mandalas are circular designs with geometric and symmetrical patterns within them. They originated in Hinduism and Buddhism. Coloring mandalas is remarkably soothing. As you color the round configurations and circles of these ancient designs, your mind can take a break and allow you to be in the present. The patterns are also repetitive, so you get into a flow of sorts. For a great coloring books of mandalas, try *The Big Book of Mandalas Coloring Book*. If you just want to find a few free coloring pages online, try www.free-mandalas.net, which offers difficulty levels and themes, or www.justcolor.net/relaxation/coloring-mandalas/, which has some challenging pages to print out.

Don't forget your crayons or colored pencils. Some people use good, old-fashioned crayons because it takes them back to childhood and it's just fun. Others opt for colored pencils as they are easier to control and more precise. Whatever you choose, they are both inexpensive.

Let the new moon be your encouragement and your inspiration to explore this new form of self-help. You can color in any moon phase, of course. See if your artwork is better under one phase of the moon than the other. On a full moon, do you color outside the lines? On a new moon, are your colors more vivid? On the back of your mandala page, write down the moon phase so you can compare if you like.

Grow Microgreens for Health

Microgreens are tiny little versions of your favorite vegetables that are clipped and harvested before they grow into larger plants. They can be grown indoors at any time of the year with little light. The new moon is a great time to plant the seeds for these greens, as it's a time of new beginnings and rebirth—and a new focus on your health can work nicely during this time.

Microgreens require little space, so you can grow them in even the smallest kitchen. They're harvested when they have four leaves and most of them will regenerate so you can continue to enjoy them. According to a February 2017 study from the *Journal of Agricultural and Food Chemistry*, they're also dense in nutrients, so a small amount does your body a world of good. In fact, studies have also shown that microgreens may help animals to lower cholesterol and protect their cardiovascular system, so there's more potential to prove that microgreens can help improve human health as well.

On top of that, they're easy to incorporate into your diet. They are easily tossed into a salad, a sandwich, added to a pizza, or even mixed into a dressing or dip. Some of the most popular microgreens include:

- Arugula
- Broccoli
- Brussels sprouts
- Cabbage
- Cauliflower
- Chia
- Endive
- Kale
- Lettuce
- Mint
- Radish
- Wheatgrass

The seeds for microgreens are different from the seeds you'd use to plant, say, a regular-sized broccoli plant (you can order them online or ask your local garden center). To plant under the new moon, you will gather your seeds, a container, and potting soil. Place the seeds into the soil, and then sprinkle a little more soil over the seeds. Water them gently—remember, they are delicate little plants and do not need to be drowned in order to grow! Place them near a window so that they receive some sunlight, but keep in mind that even in the lowest light, most microgreens will eventually grow. Placing them near a window also allows the plants to absorb moonlight.

Now, under the sliver of the new moon, you can set an intention for the growth and use of the microgreens—something along the lines of, "Under the glow of this new moon and with its increasing energy, may these seeds grow and be used for better health and powerful spiritual work." When you harvest the plants, remember to give thanks and set an intention for their continued growth and your continued health.

Create a Sacred Space for Your Spiritual Work

It's very comforting to have a special place inside your home to go to if you are doing spiritual work. Your spiritual work might include praying, reading tarot cards, doing mantras, saying affirmations, or any ritual that relaxes and soothes you. Some will call it an altar, and some may just refer to it as a peaceful place. It doesn't matter what you name it. What matters is what's on it.

The new moon phase is a time to set a foundation for things that will come or be reorganized. It is activation time. If you have a sacred place already and it needs a bit of refreshing, start at this phase. If you don't have an area that is special, now is the time to fashion one according to your needs.

Start with a dresser, table, shelf, bookshelf top, or some area you can make your own. The size needs to be determined by what you intend on doing. Think about it first. Spend time in thought and designing. The better your space, the better you will concentrate.

Once you have found your space, all you have to do it set it up in a way that suits you and makes you thoughtful and happy. Following are a few ideas:

- Candles (see color options)
    - **White:** Purity, newness, healing. Note that white is your go-to candle if you have no choices.
    - **Black:** Release and banish.
    - **Blue:** Peace, commitment, tranquility.

- **Brown:** Stability, household protection, telepathy.
- **Silver:** Deactivates negative forces.
- **Green:** Success, defuses jealousy, money.
- **Orange:** Energy, organization, self-control.
- **Pink:** Love, romance, friendship.
- **Purple:** Wisdom, psychic pursuits, power.
- **Red:** Sexual passion, physical strength, fertility.
- **Yellow:** Attraction, allure, action.
- Incense
- Wands
- Gemstones or crystals
- Statues
- Chalices
- Essential oils
- Moon phase pictures
- Paper and pen
- White sage to clear out negative energy
- A bell (Some people ring a bell as a form of protection to keep away negative vibrations. Bells are also used to signify the beginning of a ceremony or to bring forth universal power.)

Place your items where they feel good to you. Use your intuition. If you have your bonsai tree on the left and it bugs you for some reason, change it around. This is the time to be creative and have fun placing things one way and then the other.

The key is to make your sacred place enchanting, where you can worship whomever you choose or just find harmony and calm.

Write Your Own Affirmations

One technique to make positive changes in your life is using affirmations. Affirmations are basically simple sentences that you can recite to implement a positive goal or thought. The words are meant to uplift you and absorb into your subconscious mind. Start by writing affirmations down. Keep in mind three basic steps:

1. **Awareness.** It's important to note how you talk to yourself. The universe gives you back what you are thinking about, so think about what you want more of.

2. **Change negative thoughts to positive.** When you say or think words like "I've got to get over my illness," you are constantly confirming to the universe that you have an illness, so you are making it worse. You are focusing on the illness. The better choice is, "I am so grateful I am becoming healthier." Another example is financing. "I don't want to always be poor." You are telling the universe that you are not only poor but will always be. The beneficial option is, "I am moving closer to financial freedom."

3. **Repetition backed with emotion.** Words without emotions are just words. You must *feel* the thought. Think about your attitude and how you would feel if you did have the different and better life you are imagining.

Here is an exercise you can do with your affirmations:

1. On the day of a new moon, write three affirmations.
2. Starting with the day or night of the new moon and twice a day afterward, preferably in the morning and evening, go to a comfortable spot alone and sit or lie down. Relax and think or say, "I am calm." When you feel relaxed, say your positive affirmation ten times out loud or to yourself. See yourself as you would be if that affirmation were to transpire. See yourself on the scale 10 pounds less, see yourself at that new job, see yourself healthy, etc. You should be smiling.
3. Now go to affirmation number two and so on. Don't do more than three affirmations in one session or you will be overwhelmed.

In a month, assess how you are getting closer to your goals. Keep going month to month until you hit your targets (and you will).

Learn and Perform Breathwork

The new moon is a time for rebirth and self-reflection, a time when the moon's glow is not readily visible to us earthlings, and its power is relatively subdued. This is a perfect opportunity for some quiet work on the self in preparation for the more powerful phases of the moon. Now is the time to check in with your thoughts and desires, and to learn to work with your own energy. One of the best ways to do this is to practice breathwork.

Breathwork can best be described as regulating your respirations to enhance your spiritual, physical, and emotional well-being. You may be thinking, "I already know how to breathe. Why would I want to learn about this?" And of course this is true; I'm going to assume that you breathe quite well without instruction the majority of the time. But breathwork is about taking this automatic activity and turning it into a ritual that serves more than just the most basic biological need.

There are some forms of breathwork that require a certified leader or coach. Breathwork began in ancient Eastern traditions, like yoga and Buddhism, and has been used for thousands of years to detach from one's mind, soothe impulsive and reactive emotional responses, and cultivate a sense of peace and well-being. The residual effects are often felt physically in lowered blood pressure, better-managed pain and other chronic issues, and improved overall energy.

Schedule some time for a breathwork session during the muted influence of the new moon. Prepare a space for yourself outdoors at night as long as the weather allows for it. It will be quite dark without any reflection of the moon, so bring along a flashlight for your safety.

- Prepare a comfortable space on a mat, blanket, or sleeping bag.
- Feel yourself settle into the ground or whatever surface you are on.
- Set an intention for your breathwork: Do you want to feel peace, do you want to explore your desires, or do you have a desire in mind that you want to bring to fruition?
- Take an initial deep breath, inhaling for as long and drawing as deep of a breath as you can. Hold it for count of four if you can, and then release. Repeat.
- If you aren't feeling deeply relaxed, adjust your breaths accordingly.

Feel your breath and your mind working together to bring about whatever you need to focus on, keeping in mind that the new moon is the time to ready yourself for the challenges ahead.

Craft and Play in a Zen Garden for Calmness

A mini desktop Zen garden is a Japanese-style dry garden that represents nature. (It's called a garden, but no watering or maintenance is required. You basically are trying to replicate where water meets land using sand or gravel with stones in a small container or tray. The sand represents water, and you can use a small mini rake to render soothing, flowing designs. With the activity of arranging the rocks and combing the sand, you automatically start to relax and are filled with a calm energy like that of the new moon. By making your own Zen garden, you are tapping into the quietness as well as starting something fresh.

Following are some ideas of how to make your own mini Zen garden at home for a desk or tabletop. If you prefer not to make our own, you can purchase one online or at a local specialty store. They will run anywhere from $5 to $20. Make sure it comes with a rake. You can add your own personal touches.

Here's what you'll need to gather in advance to make your own:

- **Container or base for your garden:** You might be able to use the lid of a plastic container, a small deep plate, or a tray with sides.
- **Decorative sand or gravel:** A craft store or shop online will stock decorative sand. The design is up to you. Want to go pink? Go pink. It's your stress reliever. The finer the sand, the better the designs you'll be able to fashion. Please don't take a bucket from your local public beach and deplete the sources Mother Nature gave to us.

- **Rocks, stones, shells, pebbles, or marbles:** These items will represent land on in your garden. Have at least three.
- **Rake:** A mini wooden rake. Search "Zen rake" online and you'll find some for about $2. In a pinch, use a small back scratcher or a fork (but the feeling is not the same).
- **Additional embellishments:** Figurines, air plants, artificial plants, tealight, or incense holder.

1. On the day or night of a new moon, when the energy is peaceful yet starting anew, make your garden. Make sure you have a quiet place to work on your garden.
2. If you want anything to be stationary, like artificial plants, you should glue them down to the base first. (I like to change things around, so I don't glue. But that's up to you.) Consider the beauty in making things uneven or off-center.
3. Add sand.
4. Place your stones or embellishments mindfully. Zen is to be mindful.
5. Use the rake to make designs that look like water waves, ripples, zigzags, etc.

Feel free to change the pattern or setup of your garden periodically. You might want to make a change every new moon.

Make New Moon Fizz Cocktails

The time to chill is over and the time to bring some sparkle has begun. Sometimes we have to set aside meditation, aura readings, yoga, and add a little fizz to our lives. A fizzy drink is basically a carbonated beverage with somewhat of an acidic twist. A new moon is basically launching intentions and fresh ideas with somewhat of a magical twist —the perfect pairing.

The new moon complements ginger, as ginger has a fiery and exuberating affect. Its spicy and peppery notes bring to mind activity and things like love and abundance.

Lime is in sync with this phase as it projects energy and excitement. Rosemary has a robust nature and a romantic fragrance. It's perfect to add to your potential lover's cocktail!

And let's admit it. After a slow pace at the dark moon, it's time to take it up a notch and bring the new moon in with a bit of cheer and a lunar libation. You can create a new fizz…even if it is in a glass. So, if you already drink fizz cocktails, here are a couple more. Or, if you have never tried one… It's new moon time.

Easy Ginger-Lime Fizz

Yields: 2 servings

12 ounces ginger beer (this is fermented but
nonalcoholic—you can make your own or purchase it)

4 ounces seltzer water

1 ounce fresh squeezed lime juice

A slice of lime for garnish

Combine all ingredients except for garnish in a pitcher or bowl.
Serve over ice.

Easy Ginger-Lime Fizz with Alcohol

Yields: 2 servings

4 ounces vodka or gin

4 ounces ginger ale or ginger beer

4 ounces seltzer water

1 ounce fresh squeezed lime juice

A slice of lime for garnish

Combine all ingredients except for garnish in a pitcher or bowl.
Serve over ice.

Paloma Fizz Non-Cocktail

Yields: 1 serving

INGREDIENTS TO MAKE A ROSEMARY SIMPLE SYRUP:

$\frac{1}{4}$ cup sugar

$\frac{1}{4}$ cup water

1 sprig fresh rosemary, coarsely chopped

INGREDIENTS FOR THE DRINK:

$\frac{1}{4}$ cup pink grapefruit juice (squeeze your own if you can)

2 tablespoons Rosemary Simple Syrup

$\frac{2}{3}$ cup seltzer water

Rosemary sprig for garnish

Grapefruit slice for garnish (cut like a crescent moon, of course!)

Crushed ice

1. To make Rosemary Simple Syrup: Add $\frac{1}{4}$ cup water and $\frac{1}{4}$ cup sugar to a small pot. Add rosemary. Let simmer and cook until all sugar is dissolved, about 2 minutes. Strain into a small, resealable container. Let cool completely.
2. To make the drink: Pour grapefruit juice and simple syrup in a collins glass, which is a tall glass on the narrow side. Stir to mix.
3. Fill glass with ice, add the seltzer water, and garnish with the rosemary and grapefruit garnish.
4. If you want to add alcohol, add a shot of tequila to the grapefruit juice!

Juicy new thoughts and flavors are a must-have new moon combo. If you haven't tried pomegranates yet, you're in for a treat. Pomegranates are a healthy fruit with a wide range of benefits, such as high antioxidant levels. The following fizzy drink has no alcohol, so spend the extra money on the high-quality, no-sugar-added, and "not from concentrate" pomegranate juice.

Easy Fizz Pomegranate Juice

Yields: 1 serving

½ cup pomegranate juice

½ cup seltzer water

Ice

1 lemon or lime wedge for garnish

Combine juice and water over ice and garnish with lemon or lime.

Now enjoy your evening and contemplate all the wonderful things you have to look forward to in this phase of your life and moon.

Chapter 5

WAXING
MOON

The waxing phase encompasses themes like pushing out of your comfort zones, nurturing with hope and optimism, tending through deeds, and enacting intentions that you imagined and envisioned in the earlier new moon phase. According to Ayurveda, as the waxing moon is replenishing light in the night sky, our bodies are rebuilding with the nourishment of the water/earth element, known as kapha. It is a time of gathering energy and strength and replenishing your immunity, sensuality, and vitality.

There is much power in the waxing moon phase as it makes its way to full. Everything is elevating. Hence, meditations, creativity, and attitude adjustments are easier to grasp with this flow of moon magic to help you along your way. If you are full moon sensitive (meaning the full moon gets you a bit nervous or you act a bit jumpy), you are better off conducting some of the full moon undertakings when the moon is waxing, a day or two before it transforms to full.

Meditate to Bring Something You Want Into Your Life

Meditation is extremely beneficial under the influence of a waxing moon. The moon is making its trek towards fullness, and we react similarly. During this phase, everything is amplifying as the moon's vibration pulls your ambition with it. You might feel more determined, have more energy, or be able to bring on your power faster and stronger. With all this additional energy propelling you forward, now is a good time to use a simple affirmation to bring forth what you want in your life.

Try this small but mighty meditation method to give your attention to something you want without forcing the results. Sometimes simply sitting and thinking about what you want and how you will feel when you get it is better than more involved meditation techniques. Some people think meditation sounds too difficult or boring, but if they were to just sit and concentrate and visualize what they wanted, they would be meditating! Experiment, but plan to meditate for at least 15 minutes. You can use more time if you feel you require it.

1. First, think about one thing you want in your life. It is very important you have a specific, purposeful intention before you start.
2. Sit upright and relaxed in a chair. Go in with an attitude of expectancy and be alert. Remove your attention from external distractions. Offer devotion to whomever it is you call your higher power. If you pray, say a prayer. If you do not pray, ask the universal life force energy that surrounds us to attune itself to you in a focused manner while you sit in meditation. Your feet should be flat on the ground and your palms upright on your legs. Close your eyes.
3. Feel your body is being enlivened by source energy. You may visualize white light around you. You may feel a tingling vibration.
4. In many meditations, you concentrate on your breathing. But for this one, you are going to concentrate on your inner words or an affirmation that means something to you regarding what you want. If you want healing, think "heal me…heal me." Only say the words when you feel like it. Don't pressure yourself to say it so many times a minute.
5. When you feel compelled to get up and back to your normal routine, do so. Pay attention to how your desire will begin to unfold before the next waxing moon.

The universe is a series of connected properties. When you attune yourself to it intentionally, the universe includes you and things you desire to come quickly in a supportive fashion.

Answer a Question with Cartomancy

Got a question for the universe? It has the answer. As the moon waxes, so does your intuitive self. You become progressively more open to universal correspondence. Answers will come quickly, as you and moon are on the same lunar frequency. As the waxing moon expands and appears as intensifying, lean toward questions that deal with development and enlargement. Such as, "Should I get that second food truck?" or "Should I spring for a larger apartment?" Put down the tarot cards for a while and try something different. This is a quick explanation of how to read regular playing cards to answer a question or two (that's called cartomancy).

Cartomancy can be very complicated, but for our uses here, I am condensing it down to just the real basics. All you will need is the waxing moon and a deck of regular playing cards. You will be using thirty-two cards. Remove jokers and all the cards numbered 2 through 6.

1. Shuffle the cards and think of your question. Spread the cards out in front of you facedown.
2. Choose three cards and put those in front of you.

Now you are going to put together a story from your three cards using the meanings that follow. Note that the complete meanings are far more complicated. For our purposes, I have shortened the translations.

Hearts:

- **Ace**: Pertains to the home.
- **King**: Man with light complexion.
- **Queen**: Woman with light complexion.
- **Jack**: Young man or woman under eighteen or a child with light complexion.
- **Ten**: Good luck, happiness.
- **Nine**: Best card in the deck. It's a *yes* or wish card. Whatever you wanted.
- **Eight**: Romance, love, commitment.
- **Seven**: A surprise. Usually a good surprise.

Diamonds:

- **Ace**: A message.
- **King**: Man with gray hair and light complexion.
- **Queen**: Woman over thirty with light complexion.
- **Jack**: Young man or woman under eighteen or a child with light complexion.
- **Ten**: Lots of money.
- **Nine**: A surprise. See cards around it.
- **Eight**: Inheritance or something given of value.
- **Seven**: Success or a gift. When this card is next to the ace of spades, (which is a *no* card) it negates it.

Clubs:

- **Ace**: Gifts, jealousy.
- **King**: Man over eighteen with medium to dark complexion.
- **Queen**: A young female with brunette hair and blue or green eyes.
- **Jack**: Young man or woman under eighteen with darker complexion.

- **Ten:** Journey or change.
- **Nine:** *For sure* card. Luck. Depends on what cards are next to it.
- **Eight:** Stress. Card of business and uncertainty.
- **Seven:** Messages, delays. Someone showing up at your door.

Spades:

- **Ace:** Trouble, death, or death of a situation (when upside down). Heartbreak.
- **King:** Middle-aged or older man with dark complexion.
- **Queen:** A female over thirty with dark hair and dark eyes.
- **Jack:** A young male or female with dark complexion.
- **Ten:** Hospital, court, school, or building.
- **Nine:** Worst card in the deck. The *no* card or negative.
- **Eight:** Trouble and things doubtful. Nighttime.
- **Seven:** Health. Could be good or bad, see other cards. Disappointment.

To do your mini reading, put the meanings of your three cards together and you should get an answer. If you get three face cards, that means a lot of people are involved; reshuffle and ask again. Let's say you asked, "Will I get the job promotion?" and you pull the ace of hearts, king of spades, and ten of clubs. You could interpret that as, "You will hear from a man about the job and you may have to move or travel if you want it."

Remember, your intuition is heightened at a waxing and full moon, so ask away!

Create an Intention Jar

Since the moon looks like it's growing, let's use it as an appeal to our subconscious to grow some goals. You can successfully plant spinach at a waxing moon, so why not intentions?

An intention jar is a place to store goals you write down. Here's what you'll need:

- **Jar with a lid:** Reuse a glass jar you've cleaned out—it can be a spaghetti sauce jar, a small jar of mushrooms, or even a mason jar. You will be only be putting five pieces of small paper in it.
- **Paper:** Any kind of paper will do. You can use fancy stationary or a piece of regular paper. Cardboard or craft paper is fine too.
- **Pen or marker:** You want this to look good. Hence, find a higher-quality pen or marker.
- **Optional:** Stickers, ribbons, paint, or anything to decorate your jar.

1. The day or night of the waxing moon, set up the area where you will be creating your intention jar.
2. Decide on five things (or fewer) you want to have come into fruition between now and the full moon, which is in approximately seven days.

3. Write the five things down as succinctly as you can. For example: If you want to get a new apartment, you might just write, "Get apartment." The important thing is that you know what you are talking about.

4. Looking at each goal, think of a one- or two-word mantra associated with each. For example, if you want to find a mate, your mantra might be, "Love." If you want to increase your financial status, it might be, "Money." (Sounds a bit material…but so what?) For health issues, it might be, "Healing." Moving? "New home." Or you could use one for all of them, such as, "Success." Write the accompanying mantra on the back of each intention.

5. Decorate your jar the way you like. You want to associate the jar with something that makes you smile. One note: Don't put a picture of a person or animal on the jar. That confuses your thoughts when you are trying to concentrate.

6. Every day, starting the day you make your intention jar, pick up each intention and say your mantra three times. Do this daily from the first day of the waxing moon until the full moon shines in all its glory. Then recite one last mantra on the full moon.

See how far you have moved toward your goal. You can continue doing this if you feel you have not gotten as far down the lunar trail as you thought. If it all was a success, make new goals for your jar.

Plant or Place a Lucky Bamboo Plant

Adding greenery to your home is a great way to bring nature and the outdoors inside with you all the time. One easy plant to grow is called *Dracaena sanderiana*—it's a plant considered lucky in the Chinese culture. It looks like bamboo, but it's not technically not. You can grow it in water or in soil. Adding this plant to your home is great way to honor the waxing moon, as with the waxing phase you are looking for long-term success and this lucky "bamboo" grows for a long time with little care.

If you purchase a container or centerpiece of lucky bamboo already set to go, pay attention to how many stalks the plant has. If you are going to buy your own stalks and put them in a vase or container, determine how many stalks are the best for your needs. Feng shui practitioners choose certain numbers of stalks to attract good ch'i or positive energy. Here is a helpful reference so you can determine how many stalks is right for you:

- **1 stalk:** Strong and prosperous life.
- **2 stalks:** Doubles your good luck and promotes love.
- **3 stalks:** A favorite as it symbolizes a long life, abundance, and happiness.
- **4 stalks:** Bad luck and negative energy. If you have four stalks together, split them to two and two or three and one. (Note: In the Chinese language, the word used as *four* sounds very similar to the word used for *death*.) Never give four stalks as a gift.

- **5 stalks:** Harmony with your emotional, spiritual, mental, intuitive, and physical self (these are the five areas the influence your life).
- **6 stalks:** Wealth and fortune; great prosperity.
- **7 stalks:** Good health.
- **8 stalks:** Riches, progress, and fertility.
- **9 stalks:** Great luck.
- **10 stalks:** A complete and fulfilled life at its best.
- **21 stalks:** Opulence and long-term good health.

If you have decided to plant a lucky bamboo, here are some tips:

- For long stalks, keep it simple and put them in a flower vase with enough water to cover the roots, and that's it. (Use distilled or bottled water, which will have fewer minerals.)
- If you want to cut down the stalks for a shorter version, put them in a container with rocks or stones on the bottom so they don't fall out. Usually a shallow dish will do. Experiment and see what appeals to you. Change the water every seven to ten days.

Here are some other things to keep mind:

- Keep the bamboo in an area that is not too hot or too cold. Don't put it on a radiator or close to a cold draft. Indirect sunlight is best. If you are planting it in soil, regular potting soil will do, and keep it moist but not too wet.
- If you are a cat owner, keep the plant in a location your cat is not allowed. This plant can be toxic to cats, so be careful.
- Prune when the moon is dark as there is less gravitational pull and the plant won't grow as fast. On the other hand, if you want it to grow fast, prune when the moon is waxing or full.

Make Chia Seed Pudding

As we use the waxing moon as a time to plant seeds of intention to nourish and strengthen our minds and spirits, so, too, can we use seeds to nourish and strengthen our bodies.

Chia seeds are very different. They're a superfood once used by Native Americans for stamina on long trips. Chia seeds are also good for your heart and can also lower blood pressure and cholesterol levels. You can find them in most well-stocked grocery stores nowadays, or online if there aren't any in your area. Make this recipe ahead of time and you'll have two breakfast servings ready to go in the morning! You'll need:

$\frac{1}{2}$ cup rolled oats (any kind will be fine)

2–3 tablespoons chia seeds

$\frac{2}{3}$ cup almond milk

14-ounce glass jar with lid
(optional; for on-the-go snacks or breakfasts)

---

1. Stir all ingredients together in a bowl and cover. Or, transfer to jar and cover.
2. Refrigerate overnight, or at least 4 hours.
3. When ready to eat, top with fresh fruit, yogurt, raisins, or another topping of your choice.

I make this delicious recipe anytime, but when the moon is waxing, the flavor bursts through those seeds for an added culinary experience.

Multiply Love by Focusing on Loved Ones

The waxing moon contains a plethora of positive, loving energy that can be used to almost any advantage you can dream up. But because it's such a warm and giving energy, one of the best uses is to focus on the ones you love during this time.

We get so busy in our day-to-day lives that most of us forget how fortunate we are to have family, friends, and significant others. We forget there was a time before we even knew the people who have come to be the most important players in our lives, and we start to take them for granted. This is just human nature. This phase of the moon is a good time to take stock of personal relationships. Make a concerted effort to show your loved ones just how much you appreciate them. This doesn't have to be expensive or complicated. Focused energy—in the form of a conversation with your kids that is completely free of electronics, or a walk with a friend, or a backrub for your sweetie—is a pretty big deal these days!

Take time to check in on friends you haven't heard from in a while. Loneliness can be a serious challenge these days, even in our so-called connected world. Sometimes the best thing you can offer someone else is the simple act of listening. You may have a friend who is struggling with a divorce, job issues, kid issues, financial problems, an illness—the list could go on. Lending that person an ear in their time of need might be just the thing that pulls them through. Never underestimate the power of simply showing you care about someone.

Elderly family, friends, and neighbors may especially enjoy having a visitor and sharing stories from their past. Let your grandmother tell you about her friends from her childhood, even if you've heard the stories a hundred times before. You're doing her a great service, and it costs you nothing more than a little bit of your time.

Of course, when you're offering compassion and love to so many others, it's important to decompress and practice self-care too. You can't pour from an empty pitcher, so make sure you're loving and kind to yourself. This includes taking time to let go of stressors you can't control, forgiving yourself for past mistakes you're hanging onto, and allowing yourself to just *be* sometimes. Yes, it's important to have goals and plans, but it's as vital to learn to listen to your body when it needs some downtime.

Remember the loving energy you draw from the waxing moon and give to others will come back to you—sometimes in unexpected ways.

Make a Nutritious Herbal Infusion

In the days prior to the full moon, when the moon and its energy are building, you may feel more energetic. There's more and more light in the sky during the night, which may seem disruptive to sleep but actually often creates a sense of urgency in people—a feeling that they want to get things done *right now*. So you may be getting less sleep as the full moon approaches, but feeling more energized.

In light (pun intended) of this mixed-up energy, you may need a nutritional boost to keep you focused and healthy, or to set things right if you're feeling offtrack. Your body needs a good supply of minerals, vitamins, carbohydrates, lipids, and amino acids to be healthy at all times, but especially now. You can make a simple herbal infusion using easy-to-find herbs, such as:

- **Nettle:** Helps to focus energy and relieve anxiety, supports kidneys and adrenals to fight fatigue.
- **Oatstraw:** Supports emotional health by soothing and supporting the nervous system.
- **Red clover:** Helps to balance hormonal levels, improve estrogen flow, and may even help with fertility issues.

- **Alfalfa**: Packed with nutrients like vitamin K, which is good for bones and blood clotting, and vitamin C, which promotes general growth and development. These vitamins will make sure your body is running at full speed during this time of increased energy.
- **Dandelion root**: Helps to cleanse the liver, which leads to feeling more energized.

To make an infusion during the waxing moon:

1. Consider your intention. What do you hope to accomplish during the waxing moon? What about in the days beyond that? Are we looking for improved health in a specific area, for example, improving your hormonal levels or wanting to counteract lethargy in the future? Now is the time to act and continue forward in the future, using this as a launch pad to set the healing in motion.
2. Choose your herb or try a combination. You can buy loose tea and even experiment with combining teas. It's fairly well known that most store-bought tea sold in tea bags is not the highest quality tea. Sometimes when we buy tea blends, they have artificial flavorings added and they can be pricey to boot! Become a DIY tea blender instead.
3. Place 1 ounce of your herb of choice into a 1-quart jar.
4. Pour boiling water into the jar. Screw the lid on and let it steep for 8–10 hours or overnight on the counter (it will eventually go down to your room temperature).
5. Pour the infusion through a strainer into a container that you can store in the refrigerator.
6. Each day, drink at least two cups, hot or cold. Add mint, lemon, or honey if you wish.
7. You can store your infusion in the refrigerator for up to 72 hours.

You can also try other nutritional supplements and supports during this time. For example:

- Vitamins D, B_6, and E all work to support your immune system.
- Omega-3 fatty acids lower your risk of heart disease, may help to boost your mood, and support memory and brain health.
- Magnesium is an essential mineral for a variety of biochemical reactions in the body.

Do some research on your own and with your doctor to find the right nutritional support for yourself. By the time the full moon hits the sky, you will have a long-term plan in place for the following lunar cycles.

Grow Your Finances

Who says you're a selfish person because you want to be financially stable? Not me. I believe in walking a spiritual path, but I also must pay my bills.

I don't go to the grocery store and say, "Many blessings on your head," and then just take my shopping cart and run out without paying! We do need money or something of value with which to barter. What's wrong with those of us who work and want a little more? Let's use the waxing moon to make our funds grow. We love a a blueberry muffin with lots of blueberries. Why not want a bank account with more green? If you are honest, fair, and don't cheat people, there's nothing wrong with that intention.

Let's try a law of attraction technique to improve your financial situation. The law of attraction states that you attract the things you think about, good or bad. Here's how to use this during this phase:

1. The day or night of the waxing moon, relax somewhere you can be comfortable.
2. Focus on what you have financially, not what you *don't* have and how you are disappointed you don't have it. Even if you have just $1 in the bank, be grateful. If you have nothing in the bank, but are getting paid soon, be grateful.

3. Think about a small amount of money you want to come into your life. You have to take baby steps. You are programing yourself and you have to be realistic. Even if you want to win the lottery, do you think you will do it that day? Probably not. But do you think you might be able to attract an extra $75 for that week? That amount is more realistic. Now take a piece of paper and write the amount you are trying to conjure up. Let's stick with that $75, for example.

4. Next, write down a date down that is ten days from the present. Don't think of anything specific, like your friend happens to owe you $75 and maybe he or she will pay you. Don't think about where the money could come from. The universal life force needs no hints or suggestions from you.

5. Put the paper in your wallet or desk drawer and take a quick look at it three times a day. Think about how you would feel it you got that money. What would you do with it? Always think of attracting money from a legitimate source. Not someone who robs and bank and drops a few bills.

When that works, try again the next waxing moon and increase the amount. Just always stay in a range that you feel is reasonable. So if you think $500,000 is reasonable for you…go for it!

Embrace Earthing

Earthing is the practice of physically connecting to the earth, for example, by walking barefoot or lying in the grass, as a means of drawing on its energy and putting it to personal use. The term *grounded* refers to connecting to your spiritual base. Oftentimes in meditation, participants imagine a root growing out of themselves down into the ground, representing the ultimate connection to Mother Earth.

The earth actually emits an electrical frequency that's transmitted fairly easily to and through us, because we are mostly water and minerals —two excellent conductors of electricity! Our ancestors were able to access this energetic field easily because if they weren't barefoot, they were wearing foot coverings made from natural materials. Nowadays, very few of us walk around without shoes—and the soles of most footwear is made from some sort of rubber, which may provide good traction, but blocks our energetic connection to the earth.

Because the waxing moon is a time of increasing energy, it's a time to try a potentially powerful exercise—earthing under the light of the intensifying moon.

This is a pretty simple practice. Choose a time during the waxing moon when it's clear and dry outside. Give yourself at least 10 to 15 minutes for meditation (you can do a walking meditation if you'd like). You won't need much of anything—just yourself. Here are some ideas for connecting with the energy from above and below simultaneously:

- **Set your intention.** What are your goals or your hopes during the time of the waxing moon?
- **Lose the shoes.** Walk barefoot in the grass, in the dirt, in

the water. Any conductive surface will give you the benefits of earthing. Surfaces like concrete or wood are not good conductors of electricity, so go ahead and wear your shoes on the sidewalk.

- **Grow a root.** If you're standing, spread your toes and feel them grip the earth. Imagine roots growing from each foot, connecting you to the earth's core.
- **No blankets needed.** If you're going to lie on the ground, really go for a full-on connection—don't place anything between you and the earth, not even a thin sheet.

Feel the energy from the earth and the moon combining in your spiritual field. Remember to end this meditation by giving thanks to both powerful entities. Recharge with this practice as often as possible —it can work with any phase of the moon!

Perform a Kundalini Yoga Routine

There are many other forms of yoga, but for our purposes, we'll be using poses from these two practices:

1. **Active flow:** A combination of several different types of yoga, named for the way that poses "flow" into one another. Also commonly called vinyasa. The waxing moon has a steady trek as it strives for being full, and its energy seems to flow quicker and easier. The active poses do the same.

2. **Kundalini yoga:** Based on awakening kundalini energy, which is thought to be coiled like a snake at the base of the spine. Like the waxing moon raises energetic vibration with its expansion, kundalini energy passes up through each chakra (energy centers in the body), exiting though your crown chakra. This is considered a purification process in yoga. As the moon waxes to full, it also makes a journey that crescendos as well. To join the waxing moon energy and kundalini yoga may make the upward passage easier.

The following poses can help you clear your mind and make room for intuition and intention. Start by trying these active flow poses. Focus on breathing into each pose and holding each for eight to ten breaths.

- **Plank:** Start by kneeling on all fours, then stepping your feet back so that you're in what looks like a push-up pose, but with your hands and elbows directly under your shoulders. Keep your body straight and stiff, like a plank.
- **Cobra:** From the plank position, inhale and lower your hips to the floor, pushing your chest up and forward. The focus should be on holding yourself up with your back muscles, and using your hands only for support.
- **Downward Dog:** Push yourself up into an inverted *V*. Make sure your toes are pointed toward the front of your mat, and try to push your heels into the ground.

Kundalini yoga is a bit more involved. Although it also incorporates poses, its focus is on the subtle body and chakras (and teaches that each of us actually have ten bodies). As such, it's an intensely spiritual practice incorporating mantras and specific hand poses as well. Let's try a basic kundalini pose called Easy Pose:

1. Sit on the floor, stretching your legs out in front of you.
2. Bend your right leg and tuck your right foot under the left leg. Bend your left leg, tucking your left foot under the right leg.
3. Tuck your tailbone underneath you and straighten your spine. Relax your shoulders, allowing each hand to rest upward on your knees.
4. Place your hands in Gyan Mudra, meaning the tips of your thumbs and the tips of your index fingers are touching, while the other fingers are straight. This is a sacred hand position also called the "Seal of Knowledge."

Sit in this pose while doing any meditation under the pull of the waxing moon. It will help bring your intention to fruition.

Indulge In Ancient Beauty Treatments

While you're enjoying the rebuilding phase of the waxing moon, why not try out some new beauty rituals based on some of the earliest aesthetic secrets?

The Ancient Egyptians were truly ingenious people. Yes, the pyramids were really something for them to crow about, but what about their cosmetics?! These people took a look at their surroundings, spotted things as common as stones and clay and said to one another, "You know what? We can use these raw materials not only to make ourselves beautiful, but to protect ourselves from the elements!" (Full disclosure: These conversations were not recorded in hieroglyphics, so this is a little bit of conjecture.)

Think about this: Whenever Cleopatra is represented in pictures, carvings, or modern-day film, her eyes are the focus of her face. Have you ever stopped to think about where her makeup came from? After all, there wasn't a Target down the street from her palace, and the Amazon she was familiar with didn't offer two-day delivery of eye makeup. No, she used crushed rocks, minerals, clay, and plants to enhance her appearance.

- Malachite and lapis lazuli was made into a paste and used for eye shadow. (In fact, Cleopatra went so far as to mix gold pyrite flecks into lapis lazuli for a full-on va-va-voom effect. Cleo was also noted to touch up her brows to make them appear fuller with the aid of scorched almonds.)

- Black kohl (made from powdered galena) was used to line the eyelids—and was used by both men and women. Kohl was also useful in keeping pesky sand flies away from Egyptians' peepers, and it's also a natural antibiotic.

During the time of rebirth and replenishing your soul under the waxing moon, take a cue from the Egyptians and experiment with your look using natural beauty products. Ask a local aesthetician to recommend a brand that's good for your skin and budget. Use it to try that winged eye liner that originated with the Egyptians, or, if that's not appealing to you, test out a new color palette.

At the very least, you can indulge in the ultimate skincare ritual that Cleopatra swore by: milk and honey. The lactic acid in the milk acts as a natural peel and exfoliant, and honey is soothing to the skin and is an antimicrobial anti-irritant. You'll need:

---

2 tablespoons raw pure honey

2 teaspoons cow or goat milk
(Don't buy low fat. You want the fat—it softens. If you want
a vegan version, use almond or coconut milk powder. The powder
contains lactic acid that also softens the skin.)

---

1. Pour the milk and honey in a small glass or ceramic bowl and stir or whisk with a fork.
2. Spread the mixture over a clean face. Wait about 10 minutes.
3. When the mask is dried, remove it with a damp washcloth, which itself is an exfoliator.

Do this once a month at every waxing moon and see a more beautiful complexion emerge. By the time the full moon is high in the sky, your own glow will be competing with its radiance!

Journal and Freewrite to Take Action

During the waxing moon, you want to focus on the people, places, situations, or things that you want *more* of. Your goals will change from month to month, from year to year, and maybe even from day to day during a waxing moon—but one thing that doesn't change is the positive energy of this lunar phase and your ability to work with it.

A good way to keep track of what you're seeking to improve is to keep a journal. Throughout this book, we've talked about journaling during different phases of the moon. When you're journaling during the waxing moon, make sure your focus is on the future—what you want to see happen. Try to ignore what has happened in the past or what has stood in your way. Keep your eye on the prize, so to speak, and write about it in such a way that if anyone read your entry, they would know there is no doubt in your mind that this particular thing is coming your way. In other words, own it. You can keep track of these goals in your journal. Here are some topics that you might want to write about increasing or improving during this time:

- **Relationships:** With your friends, spouse, children, coworkers.
- **Income:** Are you looking for a new job or a side gig to help make ends meet?
- **Health:** Purchase healthier foods or start a new exercise routine that you enjoy.

- **Appearance**: Have you been itching to try a new cut, color, or beauty treatment?
- **Hobbies**: This is a good time to explore your interests— visit that museum you've been reading about, take a lesson in dance or music, go to a concert under the moon and stars!

Freewriting is a different way to work out your thoughts about these topics. This is unstructured, timed, and requires an open mind and free-flowing ideas. The idea behind freewriting is to get as many thoughts out of your head and onto paper as you can during the time allotted (usually 10–15 minutes). When you read through what you've written, you'll likely think, "Wow—this is all gibberish! What was I thinking??" But between those odd thoughts and ramblings, you'll find kernels of truth to cling to and expand on in your formal journal or in your meditations. Freewrite on your goals during the waxing moon and just keep writing, even if you feel stuck.

Remember that the moon is returning to its full energy during this time. Hitch your wagon to this power and hang on for the ride!

Refresh Your Hair and Nails

The waxing moon is a time to make new things happen and to get fresh perspective by drawing on new energies. This is the perfect time to take stock of your hairstyle. Lest you think this is a frivolous endeavor, consider that your hair is one of the first things people notice about you, and it can make quite the statement before you even say a word. A new shape, color, or style can completely change not only the way others perceive you, but also the way you present yourself. When your hair looks great, you feel your best, and you come across as positive, confident, and completely sure of who you are. You could also consider trying a different hair color. Try out a funky hue if it suits your mood (the worst that can happen is that you decide it's not you after all)!

Don't forget about your nails during this time of energetic expansion. If you usually take care of your nails at home, try treating yourself to a professional mani-pedi during the waxing moon. Let someone pamper you during this time of regeneration. Part of the service is usually a massage of the hands and feet, which works to improve your circulation and help you to relax. Regular mani-pedis during this moon phase also improve the health of your nails by eliminating the chance for nail fungi to take root. Rough, dry skin is soothed and prevents cracks where infections can sneak into your system.

Nail color is a simple, quick, and easy way to change up your look and your mood. You can go with the traditional reds, maroons, or French manicure, or you can add bling and zing in the form of appliques or patterns. Bring a friend along and make an afternoon out of it. Go ahead—indulge yourself, and then revel in your renewed energy.

Increase Plant-Based Protein Consumption

Why not use the waxing phase to boost your immune system and protein consumption? After all, you'll need extra energy to deal with the upcoming full moon energy. One great way to increase protein consumption is to eat shiitake mushrooms, which are native to Asian countries. They are low in calories and high in protein and B vitamins. They boost our brain function and increase energy. Plus, mushroom growth tends to be more robust by the light of the waxing and full moons. This recipe will start your day off on the right foot.

Spinach and Mushroom Frittata

Serves 6

2 tablespoons olive oil

1 medium yellow onion, diced

3 cups sliced shiitake mushrooms

2 cloves garlic, minced

4 cups chopped fresh spinach

$\frac{1}{4}$ cup chopped fresh basil

8 eggs

1 cup grated Monterey jack cheese

1 teaspoon grated nutmeg

Salt and pepper to taste

1. Preheat oven to 350°F. Coat a casserole dish lightly with pan spray or olive oil.
2. Heat oil in a large sauté pan over medium heat. Add onions and cook until tender.
3. Add mushrooms and garlic and cook until browned.
4. Add spinach and continue cooking until wilted.
5. Remove from heat, add basil, eggs, cheese, nutmeg, salt, and pepper. Transfer prepared dish. Bake in oven for 30 minutes until firm and golden brown.

Nurture an Attitude of Gratitude

When you give attention to something in your life, you get more of it. Whether the topic is love, work, or health, whatever you think about will increase. That's why the waxing moon is a perfect time to think in terms of gratitude. As the moon waxes, so will your intention. Gratitude is like magic. It will help you realize what abundance you have, here and now!

At the next waxing moon, try this gratitude exercise:

1. Jot down in a journal or on a nice piece of paper a list of things for which you are grateful. You should be grateful for a lot. Be grateful you have the eyes to read this book or the ears to hear the audio. Daily, my husband and I get up in the morning and tell each other that we are so grateful we have a home and each other. I am grateful for this book and for those who are reading it.

2. Put your writing outside or near a window where the moonlight can shine its approval upon your words. Get fancy and put it in a bottle or jar. Go as far as decorating your jar if you like. (Can't see the moon and can't go outdoors? No worries. Set it in a place of dignity that feels good to you and take a few minutes to visualize the moon shining down through the roof or window. The moon knows how to sneak in. She will be grateful, too, that you are paying honor to her influence.)

This activity can help you stay focused on the positive. If you don't, you may find more negative things happening to you. A friend of mine said recently that he has a terrible life. He has the worst luck. People treat him so badly. You know the type? It's never his fault. I asked him a simple question: "What's something good that happened today?" He said, "Nothing. I can't pay my bills, I don't have a girlfriend, and I am losing my hair."

"Well, there must be *something* good that happened," I replied.

He said, "Nope."

I responded, "What about the fact that I'm your friend and came over here today? What about the fact that you can speak, stand, and swallow? You have more than many." He grunted and uttered something like, "Yeah…well."

What he didn't notice was that he was dwelling on all the negative. By doing that, he was unknowingly increasing the number of negative things in his life. When you appreciate what you have, it puts out a positive vibe into the universe. That vibration will snowball as you appreciate more and more of what you have. When you appreciate something, it should make you feel pretty good and maybe even put a little smile on that wonderful face of yours. The more smiles and happy thoughts you have, the faster you will move from down in the dumps to feeling better. Before you know it, you will be in a much better place—all because of gratitude.

To whomever or whatever you see your higher power as, give thanks. Put out that vibration to the universe that you are looking for more good things and will get it.

Carry Quartz

All gemstones have a different frequency. Some promote healing, while others provide love or protection. During the waxing moon, let's draw special attention to clear quartz crystals, which are one of the most powerful gemstones.

Quartz vibrates at a set frequency when an electrical current is applied. Quartz is actually an important component to cell phones—it delivers a base frequency for phone calls. It also receives and transmits radio waves. Without quartz crystals, the computer age would never have happened: They are present in electronic chips and integrated circuits. Quartz is not just a passive stone in a new age pendant or something to put on your coffee table—it distributes energy.

But the power of crystals goes far beyond the products we have derived from them. They are important tools with the ability to focus and direct energy to specific intentions. Clear quartz stimulates healing and balances the elements to fulfill you and make you whole. A clear quartz crystal will also help intensify the power of any other gemstones with which it is used. Below is a brief list of the attributes of certain gemstones. As with other crystals, you can wear them in jewelry form, put them in a pocket or purse, or have them in view on a dresser or shelf. Here are some popular crystals that work well with quartz:

- **Garnet**: Promotes passion, vitality, and good health.
- **Carnelian**: Good for blood detox, aids in sexual function, and promotes positive outcomes.

- **Citrine:** Can lift your mood and feelings of self-worth. Aids in digestion and circulation.
- **Dumortierite:** Helps you retain information. Good for people studying in some way. Helps organizational skills.

When working with any gemstone, you should clear it first of anyone else's energy or any energy it may have absorbed. There are several ways to clear crystals, but the easiest is to put it in water and visualize the stone's former energy (even if it's new to you) being washed away. Then wipe it with a clean cloth. In a pinch, you can sweep your hand over the stone in the western direction and "see" the energy removing itself. (The sun goes down in the west, and that's a good path for the old energy to rest and disappear.)

As you wear or place these gemstones on your body, think about the vibration they emit and what it is you want. You can also simply hold it in your hand. Example: If you want love to come knocking, hold your garnet (raw or polished) and think about the type of person you want to come into your life. See his or her physical attributes, personality, and anything else that is important to you in a partner. If you meditate, you can wear it or put it in front of you while doing such. Research other types of gemstones, as quartz partners well with all, and see if there are others that suit your desires.

When you pair gemstones with quartz—whether on a necklace, next to each other on a table, or hanging from a place in a room that is special to you—you are enhancing the qualities of the particular stone you have chosen. It's like adding chili powder to a recipe that is already delicious, but you somehow feel needs a bit more *oomph*. Use your intuition when you hold the gemstone in your hand. If it somehow feels weak to you, include a quartz crystal. You *will* be able to feel the difference, especially when the moon is waxing and your psychic senses are on the rise. Take advantage of this phase, and use the energy of the waxing moon and clear quartz to multiply the vibrational power of these stones.

Take a Ritual Bath to Put Plans in Motion

When the moon is in transit toward its full glory, its energy is increasing. Its effects on the earth and on each of us are a little more perceptible with each passing night. Now is the time to try new projects, change your style, or put effort into any changes you envision for your life. The waxing moon is a time of increase, which means that your focus should be on the things that you want to improve upon or bring into your life. (The time to think about the things you want to cut from your life is coming during the waning moon.)

Instead of saying, "I don't want to be broke anymore," say, "I want a pay raise this month." Instead of thinking, "I'm afraid to go on a blind date," try, "I want to meet a nice person to spend time with." In both examples, the first thoughts are based on what you don't want, and the second thoughts focus on what you *do* want.

To set an intention during the nights of the waxing moon, perform a therapeutic bath ritual. You can customize it to your preferences, but it might look like this:

1. During the first night of the waxing moon, create an energy altar using candles, flowers, stones, gems, or anything found in nature that calls to you and sparks your soul.

2. Light colored or scented candles in your bathroom as you prepare for your bath. Orange is a color that represents vibrancy, joy, and stimulation, which makes it a good color for this phase of the moon.

3. Plan to soak in the tub two nights in a row. The first night will be a cleansing bath. Toss in a handful of Epsom salt, which will draw out toxins from your body, and add essential oils to purify your spiritual energy. (Cypress, lemon, lavender, and frankincense are good choices.) This bath can be a time for you to reflect on what you want to increase during the waxing moon. When you're finished, give yourself a good rinse to clear out residual negative energy and toxins.

4. The second night of soaking is to amplify your energy to put it in sync with the waxing moon's. Put a few drops of orange, eucalyptus, cinnamon, peppermint, or rosemary essential oil into your bath. This is a night for planning. Think about how you're going to put your plan into motion. After you dry off, note your thoughts in your journal or try a freewriting session.

You can also use a diffuser with energy-increasing oils throughout the day. Place it in your living room, work space, or bedroom to feel the effects of aromatherapy throughout the waxing moon.

Reconnect and Network

When the moon is coming into full power, it's a good time to forge new connections or reconnect with old pals. Introverts should especially take note at this time, as they may find it easier to put themselves out there in social situations.

Think about having a night in with your friends as a time to catch up and nourish your souls. It can be a small gathering if you like, or, if you want to really magnify and reflect the lunar energy coming into play, invite a larger, lively group. Take care to include friends who will add to the positive energy and augment the good vibes you're looking to create. You may want to work on a whole theme here by including recipes from this chapter or even a game or two.

If you have relationships that have fallen by the wayside or that are on life support, this is the time to reinvigorate them. Contact those friends and loved ones you've been thinking about and invite them to join you for a cup of tea or a glass of wine.

Because this is a period of rebirth and reenergizing, it's also a good time to get to know new people. This can be challenging for adults—after all, our worlds get smaller as we get older, and meeting new friends can be tough. The waxing moon is the perfect time to try an online site like *Meetup,* which lists activities and interests, along with upcoming gatherings of like-minded people. This is a terrific way to network, give and share advice, and develop new hobbies. You might finally be able to do things you were too afraid to try alone (like hiking in the woods or sailing, for example), or find new friends to participate in your favorite activities, like painting or going to ball games. Maybe there's a dance or music group you'd like to try out. You could end up dancing in the moonlight!

This is also a great time to search for your soulmate, as your charisma will be off the charts right now. It could be the perfect time to try an online dating service. Let your light shine freely, and let it come back to you in the form of a new love.

And don't forget about business relationships. Market yourself, network, and glad-hand like crazy right now. Your efforts will pay off handsomely!

Clear Blockages in Your Chakras

As we discussed in the Align Your Chakras to Let Go of Negative Energy entry in Chapter 2, your chakras are seven points along the spinal column that direct your life force, also known as *prana* or ch'i. Think of these points as spinning wheels or gears. If one of the wheels gets stuck or stops turning for whatever reason, the others experience a decrease in flow as well. The waxing moon is a good time to troubleshoot and find out where the blockage is so that order can be restored. It heightens our senses and moves energy faster. Let's briefly go over the seven chakras and signs that they may be blocked:

- **Root chakra:** At the base of your spine, responsible for the feeling of being grounded. This is your instinct for survival, and when it's blocked, it feels as though you're in fight-or-flight mode all the time. When it's blocked, you might feel anxious, scared, have recurring nightmares, or worry endlessly about everything.
- **Sacral chakra:** Below your belly button, associated with healthy sexuality and creative forces. When all is well, you're feeling at the top of your game—friendly, connecting with your significant other, churning out artistic work. When it's blocked, your libido disappears, and you have zero desire to create. You might feel depressed or simply lost.
- **Solar plexus chakra:** In the area of the abdomen, responsible for your self-esteem and feeling of personal power. When this chakra is not working, you'll doubt yourself and

have that sense of not being good enough. You might shy away from promoting yourself at work, for example, or allow others to treat you badly.

- **Heart chakra**: Centered in your chest, the headquarters of love. This chakra is all about wanting what's best for yourself, others, and the entire world. When it's blocked, you feel shut off, afraid to connect, and perhaps even bitter.
- **Throat chakra**: In the neck, responsible for being able to express oneself. When this chakra is blocked, you may feel as though you aren't being heard by others, or that you're having a hard time finding the right words to explain your thoughts.
- **Third eye chakra**: Centered on the forehead, provides intuition. A blockage comes across as difficulty in concentrating or an inability to understand information. You might even feel dizzy or confused.
- **Crown chakra**: Top of the head, our connection to our highest selves. Being blocked at this chakra leads to a feeling of complete disconnection to everyone and everything.

There are a variety of ways to clear blocks, including using healing crystals or simply engaging in regular meditation. If you go to an energy healer when the moon is waxing, they should be able to locate and move the energy blockage faster. If you want to clear your own block via meditation, you can visualize each chakra spinning simply and methodically in your body. Or, try visualizing the color that identifies that chakra and see it shooting into your body and reviving the chakra. Chakras that are blocked can become darker in color as the waxing moon is becoming brighter and brighter every day till it's full.

Whether you or someone else clears your energy centers, the waxing moon will sync up with your intention to unblock and lift that jammed field and allow your essence to flow. Once you've gotten the gunk out of the system, your energy will flow smoothly again and you'll be ready to take on the next phase of the moon—and your life!

Try Strength Training

As the moon is increasing in strength every night of the waxing phase, you should focus on your own strength too. We've talked about a lot of ways to practice self-care and love for others during this phase. Now let's tackle your physical strength! Even if you haven't exercised in years, you can ease into a new fitness program, no sweat. Set a goal to be a little stronger than you were yesterday. The waxing moon is a great time to begin. It's a clean slate that becomes more invigorated with each passing day.

For a heavier-duty workout, you can try either lifting weights or doing body-weight strength training. These can be done at your own pace and on your own schedule. If you need more structure to your workout or if you like others to hold you accountable for showing up, try joining a gym. You can choose from fitness classes or work out on the machines. Get a friend to join with you so that you have a fitness buddy. This is a nice option especially for people who live in colder climates and spend much of the year indoors. (If you can find a gym with a pool, you can do water aerobics but close your eyes and pretend you're in a tropical setting!)

If you don't want anyone watching you sweat, do your workouts in your own home. Free weights are fairly inexpensive and can be used to do a variety of moves, like biceps curls, dead lifts, and overhead shoulder presses. Don't be embarrassed to start light, with just 2–3 pounds at first, because you definitely don't want to hurt yourself and prevent further workouts.

Try lunges, squats, burpees, crunches, and push-ups at your at-home workout. Look at the countless free workout videos online and find one that matches your skill level and interests. If you rotate your exercises, you can have a fresh routine every day of the week. Here is a simple resistance workout based on advice from BronCoreFitness.com. You'll need:

- Floor mat
- A pair of dumbbells at a weight appropriate for you

1. First, do a warmup of:
    - 1 minute jumping jacks
    - 1 minute wall sit (stand with your back against a wall and slowly lower yourself until it seems like you're sitting on an imaginary chair)
    - 1 minute plank hold (lie in a pushup position and extend your arms to push your body off the ground)
    - 1 additional minute jumping jacks

2. Then, do this series of exercises three times.
    - 15 cross crunches (each side, for your core)
    - 20 dumbbell front squats (for your lower body)
    - 10 push-ups (for your upper body)

Muscles help with everything from posture to resting metabolism rate, so the better shape you're in, the better you'll feel, no matter what phase of the moon!

ACKNOWLEDGMENTS

I must make mention of all those who helped me create this book for you!

All the editors at Simon and Shuster, especially Eileen Mullan and Laura Daly. Oh, that Laura is such a gem!

My family: First on my mind, Bob Irwin, who so unselfishly helps others. My sister Marie, John, Daniel, Lori, Joshua, and Ethan. You too, Jax! Love you all.

My mother, Rosemarie, who made unselfish sacrifices so my sister and I could move forward.

My husband—yes, I have one and he's a keeper—Adrian Volney. My Caribbean wonder, who puts the lime in the coconut.

Bron Volney, owner of BronCoreFitness.com. Thank you for your contribution!

Christine Huynh, a true lady and fellow tea drinker who is always supportive.

Shane Volney, MD, in love and light, I thank you.

Myka, Marco, and Valentina Meier, a lovely family.

My friend, Shelly Hagen, who read many drafts and offered valuable suggestions.

Chris Shake and Christine Soderbeck, my dear friends. Oh, she won't like it that I put his name first, but he bribed me with smoked fish!

Jackie Reynolds of NY, who is talented, young, and beautiful, but one of the oldest souls I have ever met!

Dr. Robin, my Florida acupuncturist, for keeping me aligned and helping me find my joy.

Janet and Steve Osterholt, who are really nature-oriented and give back to the planet.

Ellen Anderson who, like the new moon, is all about new beginnings. Dennis gives his approval.

David Stahl, my favorite Sarasota artist and friend.

Kim Kruysman in Englewood, Florida, for your contributions to the yoga sections of this book.

Deanna Fritz, for keeping my website alive and well.

Blessings to all!

ABOUT THE AUTHOR

DIANE AHLQUIST is an author and speaker and has had a long career counseling and advising people on their spiritual questions and needs. She believes in all religions that preach no harm to anyone (including oneself), and that one should be kind and help the planet prosper. Whether or not one is religious, she believes that spirituality is the key to happiness. Diane has also worked with investigators and as a consultant for *The Blair Witch Project Dossier* by Penguin Putnam, Inc. She has been featured on *Elite Daily*, Latina.com, LunaLunaMagazine.com, iHeartRadio, and SpiritualityHealth.com. She is the author of *Moon Spells*, *Moon Magic*, and *The Law of Attraction: Have the Abundant Life You Were Meant to Have*. Her hobbies include designing and crafting jewelry, cooking, decorating, praying, and meditating.

INDEX

Abundance, attracting
   during full moon, 33–35, 45–46
   during new moon, 186
   during waxing moon, 199–200,
     220–21
Affirmations
   during new moon, 178, 180–81
   during waning moon, 88–89
   during waxing moon, 192–93
Angels, summoning, 106–7
Artistic pursuits, 15, 19–20. *See also*
   Creativity
Aura
   during dark moon, 119–20
   during full moon, 49–51
   during waning moon, 98–99
Ayurvedic spices, 93–95

Balance
   during dark moon, 111–12, 121–22,
     131–32
   during full moon, 27–29, 33–34
   during new moon, 154–55
   during waning moon, 91–92, 96–97
   during waxing moon, 204–5, 222–23
Bamboo plants, 199–200
Beauty treatments, 30, 213–14, 217. *See
   also* Skin care
Body language, 54–55
Boundaries, setting, 141–43
Breathwork, 80–82, 182–83

Candle rituals, 144–45
Cards, reading, 178, 194–96
Career/job
   during dark moon, 104–5
   during full moon, 19–20
   during new moon, 150–51, 166–67
   during waning moon, 100–101

   during waxing moon, 215–16
Cartomancy, 194–96
Chakras, clearing, 96–97, 211–12,
   228–29
Chia seed pudding, 201
Clutter, clearing, 61, 84
Cocktails, making, 186–89
Co-creation, 164–65
Contemplation, 103, 111–12, 133–36,
   144–45
Creativity
   during dark moon, 125–26, 139–40
   during full moon, 15, 19–20, 47,
     52–53
   during new moon, 156–57, 164–67,
     174–75, 178–79
   during waxing moon, 191, 215–16

Dark moon, 102–45
   angels during, 106–7
   aura during, 119–20
   balance during, 111–12, 121–22,
     131–32
   candle rituals during, 144–45
   career/job during, 104–5
   contemplation during, 103, 111–12,
     133–36, 144–45
   creativity during, 125–26, 139–40
   dreams during, 113–14
   energy during, 103–12, 119–23,
     131–32, 139–45
   fasting during, 115–16
   feng shui during, 109
   fortune telling during, 130
   healing baths during, 108–10, 123–24
   healing crystals/gemstones during,
     111–12
   healing foods during, 123–24
   higher powers during, 104–5

New Moon—*continued*
  cocktails during, 186–89
  co-creation during, 164–65
  creativity during, 156–57, 164–67,
    174–75, 178–79
  energy during, 148–59, 162–65,
    182–86
  feng shui during, 156–57
  finances during, 150–51, 180–81
  green lifestyle during, 172–73
  growing microgreens during, 176–77
  healing baths during, 152–53, 168–69
  healing crystals/gemstones during,
    154–55
  healing foods during, 160–61, 176–77
  herbal remedies during, 152–53,
    170–71
  higher powers during, 164–65
  journaling/freewriting during, 166–67
  kindness during, 158–59
  launching ideas during, 147–49
  mandalas during, 174–75
  meditation during, 148–49
  power of, 11, 13, 146–89
  relationships during, 170–71, 186
  skin care during, 152–53, 168–69
  smudging techniques during, 162–63
  tea ceremony during, 170–71
  walks during, 150–51
  workspace during, 156–57, 178–79
  yoga routine during, 182–83
  Zen garden during, 184–85
Numerology, 133–36

Partner, attracting, 23–24
Past-life regression, 117–18
Pendulum, using, 131–32
Plants, growing, 41–44, 127, 176–77,
  199–200
Problems, releasing, 87–88, 96–97,
  144–45
Protein consumption, 218–19

Reconnections, 226–27
Relationships, improving
  during full moon, 23–24, 41–42,
    52–53
  during new moon, 170–71, 186
  during waning moon, 61, 68–69,
    80–82, 96–97, 100–101
  during waxing moon, 202–3, 215–16,
    226–27
Remote viewing, 128–29

Saltwater remedy, 72–73
Self-care rituals, 56–57, 83, 137–40
Shadow work, 113, 139–40
Skin care
  during dark moon, 108–10, 123–24
  during full moon, 30
  during new moon, 152–53, 168–69
  during waning moon, 70–79, 85–86
  during waxing moon, 213–14, 217
Slowing down/relaxing, 62–63
Smudging techniques, 162–63
Spiritual workspace, 178–79
Strength training, 230–31
Stress, releasing, 62–63, 80–82, 91–92,
  125–26

Teas, herbal, 170–71, 204–6
Toxic people, avoiding, 66–67
Trees, planting, 41–42

Unions, celebrating, 41–42

Vegan foods, 160–61
Vibrational energy, 23–26

Walks, taking, 150–51, 209–10
Waning moon, 60–101
  affirmations during, 88–89
  aura during, 98–99
  Ayurvedic spices during, 93–95
  balance during, 91–92, 96–97